CHICOPEE PUBLIC LIBRARY
449 Front Street
Chicopee, MA 01013

CH **WITHDRAWN**

W9-AZV-784

NOV 9 5

CHICOPEE PUBLIC LIBRARY
MARKET SQUARE
CHICOPEE, MA 01013

SCIENTIFIC
AMERICAN *SOURCEBOOKS*

THE WORLD OF
ATOMS
AND QUARKS

ALBERT STWERTKA

JNF : 539.7 STWERTKA

TWENTY-FIRST CENTURY BOOKS

A Division of Henry Holt and Company
New York

• For Alexander and Carolyn •

Twenty-First Century Books / A Division of Henry Holt and Company, Inc. / *Publishers since 1866*
115 West 18th Street / New York, NY 10011

Henry Holt ® and colophon are trademarks of Henry Holt and Company, Inc.

Henry Holt and Company, Inc., and Scientific American, Inc., are both wholly owned subsidiaries of Holtzbrinck Publishing Holdings Limited Partnership. Twenty-First Century Books, a division of Henry Holt and Company, Inc., is using the Scientific American name under a special license with that company.

Text Copyright © 1995 by Albert Stwertka
All rights reserved.
Published in Canada by Fitzhenry & Whiteside Ltd.
195 Allstate Parkway, Markham, Ontario L3R 4T8

Library of Congress Cataloging-in-Publication Data
Stwertka, Albert./The world of atoms and quarks / Albert Stwertka. – 1st ed.
p. cm. — (Scientific American sourcebooks). Includes bibliographical references (p.) and index.
1. Nuclear physics—Juvenile literature. 2. Atoms—Juvenile literature. 3. Atomic theory—Juvenile literature. 4. Particles (Nuclear physics)—Juvenile literature. [1. Atoms. 2. Atomic theory. 3. Nuclear physics.] I. Title. II. Series.
QC778.5.S79 1995   539.7—dc20   95–936

ISBN 0–8050–3533–8 (hardcover) / ISBN 0–8050–3534–6 (paperback)
First Edition 1995

Printed in the United States of America
All first editions are printed on acid-free paper ∞.
10 9 8 7 6 5 4 3 2 1

Design by Kelly Soong

Photo Credits
p. 5, 7, 18, 40, 43, 52: Science Photo Library/Photo Researchers, Inc.; p. 9, 15, 49, 55, 69: Lawrence Berkeley Laboratory/Science Photo Library/Photo Researchers, Inc.; p. 10: Dr. Jeremy Burgess/Science Photo Library/Photo Researchers, Inc.; p. 16: Van Bucher/Photo Researchers, Inc.; p. 19: Chris Bjornberg/Photo Researchers, Inc.; p. 20, 21: courtesy AIP Niels Bohr Library; p. 23: Brookhaven National Library/Science Photo Library/Photo Researchers, Inc.; p. 25, 86, 89, 93: Ken Eward/Science Source/Photo Researchers, Inc.; p. 26: University of Oxford, Museum of History and Science/courtesy AIP Niels Bohr Library; p. 30: Société Française de Physique, Paris/courtesy AIP; p. 31: Mehau Kulyk/Science Photo Library/Photo Researchers, Inc.; p. 35: C. Powell, P. Fowler and D. Perkins/Science Photo Library/Photo Researchers, Inc.; p. 37: Fritz Reiche Collection/courtesy AIP Niels Bohr Library; p. 44, 62, 63, 66, 81: David Parker/Science Photo Library/Photo Researchers, Inc.; p. 46: Photo Researchers, Inc.; p. 50: photograph by Francis Simon/AIP Niels Bohr Library; p. 51: Science Source/Photo Researchers, Inc.; p. 59: University of Chicago/courtesy AIP Niels Bohr Library; p. 60: Patrice Loiez, CERN/Science Photo Library/Photo Researchers, Inc.; p. 61: Carl Anderson/Science Photo Library/Photo Researchers, Inc.; p. 72: Harvey and Pasedena/courtesy AIP; p. 73: Philippe Plailly/Eurelios/Science Photo Library/Photo Researchers, Inc.; p. 74, 76: Michael Gilbert/Science Photo Library/Photo Researchers, Inc.; p. 78: Hank Morgan/Science Source/Photo Researchers, Inc.; p. 82: Superconducting Super Collider Laboratory/Science Photo Library/Photo Researchers, Inc.; p. 94: Clive Freeman, The Royal Institution/Science Photo Library/Photo Researchers, Inc.

CONTENTS

ONE
Atomos
5

TWO
The Periodic Table
9

THREE
Cutting the Atom
15

FOUR
The Nuclear Atom
23

FIVE
The Quantum World
35

SIX
Waves of Matter
43

SEVEN
Quantum Numbers
49

EIGHT
The Particle Explosion
55

NINE
The Standard Model
69

FOR FURTHER READING
83

PERIODIC TABLE OF ELEMENTS
84

PARTICLE GUIDE
86

GLOSSARY
89

PHOTO NOTE
93

INDEX
94

ONE

ATOMOS

What is matter made of? Today scientists are convinced that our whole complex world is made up of only a few basic building blocks called atoms. There are different kinds of atoms, of course, but a fairly small number of atoms account for the almost unlimited variety of materials existing all around us. The fact that matter comes in tiny chunks with empty space between them is one of the most important discoveries in all of science. Although this is a very ancient idea, it took twenty centuries to confirm it.

The word *atom* comes from the Greek word *atomos*, usually translated as "indivisible," or "undividable." As early as 400 B.C., the Greek philosopher Democritus (c. 460–c. 370 B.C.) and others asked a simple question: What happens to a material such as silver when it is cut in half? You obviously end up with two pieces of silver. But suppose you keep cutting the silver into smaller and smaller pieces. Is there a limit to how small a piece of silver you can have? Democritus and his disciples reasoned that there must be a limit: a smallest piece of silver, an "atom" of silver, that could no longer be cut. Democritus wrote, "The only existing things are atoms and empty space; all else is mere opinion."

It's important not to read too much into the early ideas of the atom. The ancient Greeks had no way of testing their ideas, and many of the properties they associated with atoms are very strange sounding and have little in common with the way modern science uses the concept of the atom today.

Democritus and his followers believed, for example, that matter was made up of four "elements"—earth, water, fire, and air. Each of these elements was made up of atoms. They were held together by Love, and even the human soul was made of "fine, smooth round atoms like those of fire."

The early Greek idea of the atom was soon ignored and forgotten. It was not until the nineteenth century, almost 2,000 years later, that the theory was taken up again. This time, however, experimental tools and techniques were available to test the theory.

DALTON'S ATOMIC THEORY

The Greek idea of the atom was revived when the study of nature became an observational science with results based on experiments. John Dalton (1766–1844) is generally considered the father of modern atomic theory.

Dalton began teaching school in Manchester, England, at the incredibly young age of twelve. He first dabbled in chemistry as a hobby, but soon established himself as one of England's leading scientists. He had an intense interest in meteorology, which is the study of the atmosphere and of the various factors that affect weather. This work led him to the theory of atoms, because he found it could explain certain properties of the gases that make up the air. In 1808 he published an important book titled *New System of Chemical Philosophy* that marked the beginning of modern chemistry.

At the time, it was already known that when a substance is analyzed by chemical means, it can be broken down into simpler and more basic forms of matter, called elements. Iron, gold, silver, oxygen, and hydrogen are all examples of elements. A substance such as water is called a compound, since it is made up of two elements, hydrogen and oxygen.

In his book, Dalton stated that atoms are the ultimate particle from which all elements are made. All the atoms that make up a typical element such as oxygen, for example, have the same weight, behave the same way in all chemical reactions, and are identical in every possible way. A different element, such as hydrogen, has atoms with weights and properties different from oxygen's. These differences distinguish one element from another.

Dalton also realized that atoms can join together to form more complicated structures with unique chemical properties. These new chemical units are called molecules. (A molecule is the smallest unit of any compound.) Finally, he stated that in any chemical change or reaction, the atoms that make up the molecules are never destroyed but are simply shuffled about and rearranged to form new molecules.

Dalton's ideas came at a time when observational research was building

A teacher, chemist, and meteorologist, John Dalton is also known as the father of modern atomic theory.

a solid foundation for chemistry. His insistence that atoms always kept their identity, and that there was no such thing as a fraction or piece of an atom in a molecule, could be quickly checked in the laboratory.

If we compare atoms to marbles, then a molecule can be thought of as a bunch of marbles that are stuck together. The important idea here is that the ratio of the different atoms that make up a molecule must be a ratio of whole numbers. For example, if you think of a make-believe molecule that is always made up of 5 green marbles and 3 red marbles, it's obvious that the ratio of green to red marbles will always be 5:3, a ratio of whole numbers, no matter how many molecules you have.

To verify this in the laboratory, a chemist simply has to take a substance such as water, known to be made up of molecules of hydrogen and oxygen, decompose it into its components, and then compare the amounts of oxygen and hydrogen that are formed.

The decomposition of water, which is made up of 2 atoms of hydrogen and 1 atom of oxygen, will always result in 2 volumes of hydrogen being produced for every 1 volume of oxygen. The results are always the same, no matter how much water is decomposed. Since 2 volumes of hydrogen contain twice the number of molecules as in 1 volume of oxygen, the result shows that 2 atoms of hydrogen always combine with 1 atom of oxygen. This simple deduction based on atomic theory is today one of the great laws of chemical combination.

Dalton's work appeared very early in the nineteenth century, and several of his ideas have had to be modified. Atoms are not indivisible, for example. You are bound to have heard of "atom smashers," whose function is to break atoms apart. The "splitting" of uranium atoms (a process usually called fissioning) in a nuclear reactor is another example of the fact that atoms can be broken apart. This breaking apart supplies the energy that is at the heart of nuclear power.

All the same, Dalton's work established atomic theory as a measurable, quantitative scientific field of study. Other scientists quickly followed his lead and began to develop new techniques to measure some of the properties of atoms. By ingenious experiments such as measuring the time it takes for two gases to mix, or by measuring how far a given amount of oil will spread when placed on the surface of water, scientists began to estimate the sizes of atoms and molecules. For one thing, they found that the size of a typical atom is approximately one-tenth of a billionth of a meter.

TWO

THE
PERIODIC TABLE

*T*he scientists of the nineteenth century constantly had to defend their belief in the existence of atoms. Since an atom was too small to be seen, there were always skeptics and doubters.

BROWNIAN MOTION   A Scottish botanist, Robert Brown (1773–1858), was the first to notice very dramatic evidence for the physical existence of atoms and molecules in a rather surprising series of observations. Looking through a microscope, he began a study of the behavior of tiny pollen grains suspended in water. He noticed that they were bouncing around in a perpetual dance. The pollen grains moved as if they were constantly being hit by tiny bullets fired at them from random directions. Brown tried various other types of fine suspensions such as particles from pulverized rock, soot, and even "London dust." The particles all zigzagged about in random motion.

This erratic motion, now called Brownian motion, is actually caused by molecular "bullets" of water, moving in random directions, hitting the tiny grains in irregular patterns and pushing them into irregular, random motion.

It was still impossible to see a molecule, but molecules had become "visible" through the numerous collisions they made. It was not until the twentieth-century work of Albert Einstein (1879–1955) that a mathematical theory for this motion was developed. We usually associate Einstein with the

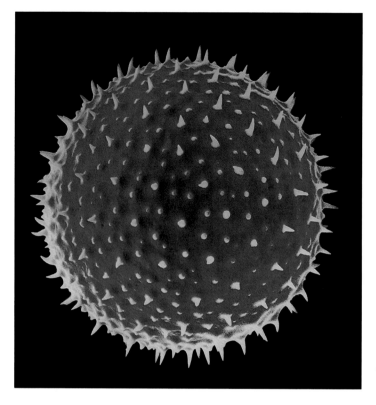

Robert Brown used the movement of pollen grains in water to prove the existence of atoms. A single pollen grain is shown here, magnified many times.

theory of relativity, but his paper on Brownian motion, published in 1905, is one of his great works.

MOLECULES   Most familiar substances, such as water, are made of molecules rather than single atoms. Molecules consist of 2 or more atoms bound together in fixed ratios to form a stable unit of a given substance. Remember, water molecules have 2 atoms of hydrogen combined with 1 of oxygen. A molecule of sugar consists of 6 atoms of carbon, 12 atoms of hydrogen, and 6 atoms of oxygen. Table salt is made up of molecules of sodium chloride. Break the molecules apart, and you always have a ratio of 1 atom of sodium to 1 atom of chlorine.

Molecules come in all sizes. Some, like the molecules of carbon monoxide, found in automobile exhaust, are small and consist of only 2 atoms. A water molecule contains 3 atoms, while a biologically important molecule such as a hormone or protein can contain thousands of atoms.

If you separate a molecule into the atoms that make it up, you no longer have the original compound. These atoms have quite different properties from those of the molecules they are part of. In the case of salt, for example, sodium is an extremely active metal, while chlorine is a greenish poisonous gas. Neither of these is something you would want to add to your food!

THE PERIODIC TABLE   Much of the history of chemistry through the ages has involved the study not only of compounds but of the products of their decomposition. At first this involved heating minerals over a charcoal fire to obtain such metals as iron, copper, and silver. Other chemical techniques were gradually developed to separate compounds into their simplest building blocks, the elements.

Scientists have discovered or created 111 different elements to date. Ninety of them are found naturally on Earth, while the rest are made artificially in laboratories throughout the world. Some of the elements are quite rare, and some are so unstable that they are called radioactive. But all of them are different from one another. All the millions and millions of substances that exist are made up of one or more of these elements.

The discovery of these elements made an immense impact on the scientific investigation of matter. It revealed an underlying simplicity to the structure of everything. But with so many elements to deal with, chemists were still faced with a jumble of chemical facts. Every element is different, with a different weight, size, and properties. Some elements, like oxygen and nitrogen, are gases, and some, like gold and platinum, are metals. Some, like carbon, readily combine with other elements to form a huge number of molecules, while some, like helium, are completely inert and combine with nothing else.

Two scientists greatly simplified our knowledge of the way atoms behave chemically. They were a Russian chemist, Dimitri Ivanovitch Mendeléev (1834–1907), and a German physicist, Julius Lothar Meyer (1830–1895). Mendeléev is usually given credit since he managed to publish his work a little before Meyer.

In preparing a chemistry textbook for his students at the University of St. Petersburg, Russia, Mendeléev wrote out the known properties of the elements on cards. Sorting through them, he noticed that when he arranged the cards in order of increasing atomic weight, certain chemical properties repeated themselves. Using the weight of the atoms as an organizing principle, he arranged the elements in rows, and then stacked the rows so that similar elements fell into the same column. This arrangement of rows and columns forms what we now call the periodic table.

Let's start with the element lithium as an example, and arrange the elements in a row according to their increasing weights. If we then start a second row by placing the element sodium under lithium, the chemical properties of the elements repeat themselves.

Li	Be	B	C	N	O	F	Ne
Lithium	Beryllium	Boron	Carbon	Nitrogen	Oxygen	Fluorine	Neon
6.94	9.01	10.81	12.01	14.00	15.99	18.99	20.18
Na	Mg	Al	Si	P	S	Cl	Ar
Sodium	Magnesium	Aluminum	Silicon	Phosphorus	Sulfur	Chlorine	Argon
22.99	24.31	26.98	28.08	30.97	32.06	35.45	39.94

The elements lithium and sodium in the first column are both silvery metals that are so reactive chemically that they burst into flames when exposed to air. Fluorine and chlorine in the seventh column are both very active yellow-green gases that have irritating odors and are poisonous. And, to take one more example, neon and argon in the eighth column are both completely inert, nonreactive gases that react with no other element.

The modern version of the table is more complicated than the very sketchy sample shown above, but the principle used to construct it is the same: the chemical behavior of the elements repeats periodically. (A complete periodic table appears on pages 84–85.)

The creation of the periodic table was extremely significant. Its strength lay not only in simplifying the study of chemistry, but in its great predictive power. Mendeléev found that in order to place each element in a row consistent with its chemical behavior, he had to leave certain spaces in the table blank. He suggested that these gaps would be filled by elements yet to be discovered, and was even able to describe in some detail what properties these elements should have. Mendeléev's predictions proved true, and within the next hundred years, all the missing elements were found.

As so often happens after great scientific breakthroughs, new questions and challenges soon followed the creation of the periodic table. A few elements, such as argon and potassium, did not fall into the right column if they were placed in the table in order of their weights. And how was it possible for a slight difference in atomic weight to change the properties of neighboring elements so radically? For example, fluorine is followed by neon and then by sodium in the table. The shift in chemical behavior as we examine these elements, one after the other, couldn't be more extreme. We have already noted that fluorine is a greenish gas that reacts violently with almost every other element, and that neon is an extremely inert gas that reacts with nothing else, while sodium is a silvery metal that bursts into flames spontaneously in air.

Until the late 1890s, nothing was known about the structure of atoms, so these problems couldn't be solved, nor could these questions be answered. Atoms were still thought of as hard grains of matter, rather like billiard balls, moving rapidly about and bouncing off one another and any other boundary they came in contact with. The first to discover anything about the internal structure of atoms was the English physicist Sir Joseph John Thomson (1856–1940), the discoverer of the electron. Modern physics begins at this breakdown of the "ancient" theory of the atom.

THREE

CUTTING
THE ATOM

When Joseph John Thomson, professor of physics and director of the Cavendish Laboratory at Cambridge University, England, announced in April 1897 that he had discovered an electrically charged particle smaller than an atom, the news was greeted with astonishment bordering on disbelief. The Cavendish Laboratory was, at the time, one of the world's leading institutions for research in physics, and any announcement by its head had to be taken very seriously. Yet, as Thomson later recalled, "I was told by a distinguished colleague who had been present at my lecture that he thought I had been 'pulling their legs.'"

ELECTRONS   However, it was true. Thomson had discovered the electron, a negatively charged particle that had a mass of approximately $\frac{1}{2,000}$ that of hydrogen, the lightest atom.

There are two kinds of electric charges, positive and negative. These names are entirely arbitrary, and the scientists who named them could just as well have called the negative kind positive and vice versa. The charged particles exert forces on each other. Objects that carry like charges repel each other, and oppositely charged objects attract each other.

Thomson's discovery was made with the aid of a gaseous discharge tube. At the time, many physicists were experimenting with this kind of tube, which consists basically of a glass cylinder containing a gas at low pressure and having two metal discs, called electrodes, sealed inside at each end.

When a high-voltage generator is connected to the electrodes, an elec-

Joseph John Thomson worked with gaseous discharge tubes to discover the electron.

tric current flows through the tube, and it begins to glow very much like the neon signs one sees in advertising displays. If the gas pressure is lowered, the glow disappears, but the tube still conducts electricity. How, then, was electricity being conducted through the tube that had so little gas in it?

Thomson discovered that one of the electrodes, the negative electrode, called the cathode, gives off invisible rays that pass through the gas and carry the electric current. He could make the presence of these rays, which he called cathode rays, visible by changing their paths with magnetic fields. By bending the paths of the cathode rays through the tube, he could make them strike the glass wall of the tube, rather than travel straight to the opposite electrode. The impact made the glass glow with a greenish bluish color.

Thomson succeeded in making careful measurements of the deflection of the cathode rays in electric and magnetic fields, and was able to establish that the cathode rays, the carrier of the electric current, behaved like small negatively charged particles. These particles were later named electrons. Where did these electrons come from? Thomson correctly guessed that they were essential parts of atoms. In his own words, "Electrification essentially involves the splitting up of the atom, a part of the mass of the atom getting free and becoming detached from the original atom."

Electrons are part of every atom, from the smallest—hydrogen—to the largest—uranium, and the artificial elements that follow uranium in the periodic table. Electrons are all identical, with the same amount of charge and mass. In spite of the reluctance of others to believe in bodies smaller than an atom, Thomson felt "that the experiment left no escape from . . . my belief in the existence of bodies smaller than atoms." Thomson was awarded the Nobel Prize in physics in 1906 for the discovery of the electron and for his work on the conduction of electricity by gases.

A PLUM PUDDING ATOM

It would seem natural that Thomson would follow his discovery of the electron with an attempt to understand its role in atomic structure. Any model of the atom had to account, first of all, for the fact that the atom is electrically neutral. Electrons have a negative charge and are part of an atom, yet the atom as a whole has no electric charge. The atom must therefore also contain something in it that has a positive charge.

If we add equal amounts of negative and positive charges together, the charges cancel each other. An object that is negatively charged can be made electrically neutral if we add an equivalent amount of positive charge.

When Thomson created his first model of the atom, he took the view that the negative charge of the electrons is just balanced by positive charge distributed more or less uniformly inside a sphere. The electrons were embedded in this cloud of positive charge like, as he put it, raisins in a plum pudding.

There remained the problem of how to account for the mass of the atom. The mass of an electron is a small fraction of the mass of an atom, and Thomson therefore first assumed that an atom must contain thousands of electrons. But this view was soon proven wrong when studies showed that atoms contained relatively few electrons. The positive charge, whatever it was, must therefore contribute the major share of an atom's mass.

MYSTERIOUS RAYS

The speed with which physics was changing during the last few years of the nineteenth century was remarkable. Approximately a year and a half before Thomson's discovery of the electron, two other important discoveries had already been announced.

In 1895 Wilhelm Conrad Röntgen (1845–1923), professor of physics at universities in Würzburg and Munich, Germany, announced his discovery of X rays. In the course of his research, Röntgen noticed that he could produce very penetrating radiation in a gaseous discharge tube by applying high voltage across its two electrodes. This radiation, called X rays, could penetrate fairly thick layers of material such as human tissue and even metal. Röntgen quickly realized the value of X rays to the field of medicine, and within weeks of the discovery he produced the first X-ray photograph of a hand. He was given the first Nobel Prize ever awarded, in 1901, in physics for his discovery. For many years X rays were called Röntgen rays in his honor.

An X-ray tube is very similar to the monitors now used for television and computers. In a tube of this kind, electrons are produced by a cathode, usually in the form of a hot metallic filament at one end. A high positive voltage applied to a metallic electrode called the anode at the other end of

A caricature published around 1900 portrays Wilhelm Conrad Röntgen, the discoverer of X rays.

the tube attracts the electrons and accelerates them to high speeds. The anode acts as a target, so it is usually made of a metal, such as tungsten, with a high melting point. When the electrons finally strike the anode, a certain percentage of their energy is changed into an intense beam of X rays.

Three months after Röntgen's discovery of X rays, in 1896, Antoine-Henri Becquerel (1852–1908), professor of physics at the École Polytechnique in Paris, France, published his first paper on radioactivity. Working with a compound of uranium, he noticed that the compound gave off radiation that could penetrate several layers of opaque paper. The paper had been used to wrap a photographic plate, and Becquerel found that the mysterious radiation had left its imprint on the film by blackening it.

The search for the source of this mysterious radiation was taken up by Marie Curie (1867–1934), one of the most extraordinary scientists of the

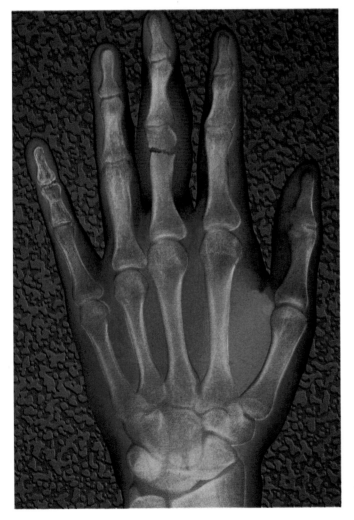

Röntgen's first X-ray photograph was of a hand. This color-enhanced X ray of a hand shows a fractured middle finger.

modern era. She and her husband, Pierre (1859–1906), discovered the same phenomenon in other elements such as polonium and radium. Both of these elements were actually discovered by the Curies in 1898. Polonium was named for Poland, Marie Curie's homeland, and it was she who suggested the name radioactivity. The Curies and Becquerel shared the Nobel Prize in physics in 1903 for their work on radioactivity. In 1911 Marie Curie was one of the rare individuals to receive a second Nobel Prize, this time in chemistry, for her work on radium and polonium.

By 1898 Ernest Rutherford (1871–1937), working at the Cavendish Laboratory in England, had discovered that there are at least two different kinds of radiation given off by radioactive elements. They are now called alpha particles and beta particles. This discovery was soon followed by the work of Paul Ulrich Villard (1860–1934), a professor of chemistry at the École Normale Superieure in France, who detected a third species of radiation called gamma rays.

*M*arie and Pierre Curie shown working together in their laboratory, in 1896.

By 1900 it was known that beta particles are electrons. It was a bit more difficult to identify the gamma rays, but it was soon realized that they were similar to very penetrating and energetic X rays. Rutherford completed the identification process by recognizing that alpha particles were helium atoms stripped of their normal complement of two electrons, so that they were emitted with a double positive charge. (An atom that has an electric charge of this kind, whether it is positively or negatively charged, is called an ion.)

Within a few years of the discovery of radioactivity, it was known that radioactive atoms are unstable atoms that can spontaneously emit electrons, helium ions, and powerful X rays. It was still very much a mystery why certain atoms are radioactive while others are stable, and which part of the atom the radiation was coming from.

Much of the progress in our understanding of the atom during the first two decades of the twentieth century is associated with Ernest Rutherford. Rutherford, who was born on a farm in New Zealand, quickly rose to

Ernest Rutherford made several major contributions to the study of atoms and their structure.

become a world figure as a scientist. His brilliant and independent thought inspired a whole generation of physicists working to understand the structure of the atom.

Rutherford's early work on the principles of radioactivity was done while he was professor of physics at McGill University in Montreal, Canada. In 1902 he and Frederick Soddy (1877–1956) discovered that when a radioactive atom emits radiation it changes itself into a different element. They called this phenomenon a transmutation of the elements. When uranium emits an alpha particle, for example, the uranium atom transmutes itself into an atom of thorium. The effect that centuries of medieval alchemy had labored in vain to achieve—transmuting one element into another—had been occurring by itself, without help from anyone.

Rutherford was awarded the Nobel Prize in chemistry in 1908, at the age of thirty-seven, for his investigations of radioactive elements. By this time, he had moved to the University of Manchester in England. It was here that he made the greatest discovery of his career—a discovery he made *after* winning the Nobel Prize.

FOUR

THE NUCLEAR ATOM

While studying the nature of alpha particles given off by radioactive atoms, Rutherford had been impressed with their penetrating power. These positively charged particles are emitted with great speed and energy and easily pass through thin sheets of glass or metal. It occurred to Rutherford that these helium "bullets" could be used to probe the interior of the atom. They could possibly penetrate an atom and give some information about its structure.

Two of Rutherford's research students at Manchester performed the crucial experiments. One was Johannes Hans Wilhelm Geiger (1882–1945), and the other was Ernest Marsden (1889–1970). Geiger later became famous for his work on a radiation detector, now usually called a Geiger counter.

In their experiment, Geiger and Marsden bombarded a target of thin foils of gold and silver with alpha particles from a radioactive radium-C source. Using a zinc sulfide scintillating screen, they observed the deflection of the alpha particles as they passed through the foils. This screen is very similar to the phosphor that gives an image in a television tube. When an alpha particle strikes the screen, a weak point of light called a scintillation is given off and makes the impact visible.

The results of the experiment were startling. Most of the alpha particles passed right through the thin foil, but about 1 in approximately every 10,000 particles was scattered at all angles, some greater than 90 degrees. Geiger reported that some were even deflected backward, like a ball bouncing off a wall.

Rutherford was fond of saying that the results were the most incredible he had ever heard of. As he described it, "It was almost as incredible as if you fired a 15-inch shell at a piece of tissue paper and it came back and hit you."

To understand why Rutherford was astonished, remember that an alpha particle has a mass that is about 8,000 times that of an electron. If the plum pudding model of the atom were correct, the alpha particle would collide with one or more of these electrons embedded in a cloud of positive charge as it penetrated the atom. It is as hard to imagine that an alpha particle could bounce back from such a collision as that a tractor would bounce back from a collision with some bicycles.

Within a year, Rutherford came up with the reason for the startling results of the experiment. In his own description of the experiment, he "realized that this scattering backwards must be the result of a single collision, and that in order to have a deflection of this magnitude, the greater part of the mass of the atom must be concentrated in a small, minute, nucleus carrying a charge."

To understand Rutherford's reasoning, consider an experiment to investigate the contents of an opaque "black" box (a box which cannot be seen into) by firing bullets at it. Most of the bullets go straight through the box, but every once in a while, a bullet goes bouncing off at a sharp angle, even coming right back at you. You would deduce that the box is mainly empty, but that it does contain a small, dense, object that can cause a speeding bullet to ricochet off at a sharp angle.

When Rutherford presented his results in the May 1911 issue of the *Philosophical Magazine*, they made a profound impact on the world of science. His announcement is often said to have given birth to the nuclear atom. Subsequent experiments showed beyond doubt that the atom consists of a small, positively charged nucleus surrounded by a cloud of negatively charged electrons.

The nucleus is extremely small, some 100,000 times smaller than the atom as a whole, but contains almost all the mass of the atom. If an atom were enlarged to the size of a house, the nucleus would be the size of a small pea placed at its center. Atoms consist mainly of empty space.

Rutherford had actually worked out the mathematics of the laws that alpha particle scattering should obey, and found that the size of the nuclear charge should profoundly affect the scattering pattern. Using this fact, sci-

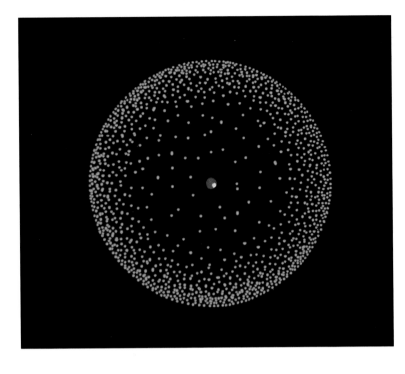

A *computer-generated graphic shows a nucleus surrounded by a cloud of electrons. Remember, scientists in Rutherford's day did not have computer graphics to help them understand the structure of atoms!*

entists conducted scattering experiments to determine the charge on the nucleus of many of the elements.

The results of these experiments led to a new way of defining an atom in terms of the charge carried by its nucleus. This charge, which is always expressed as a whole number of charges, such as 1, 2, 3, is called the atomic number of an element, and is always referred to as Z.

The measurement of atomic numbers for all the elements presented a major experimental challenge that was brilliantly met by Rutherford, aided by his young assistant Henry Gwyn-Jeffreys Moseley (1887–1915).

ATOMIC NUMBERS   Moseley was a gifted physicist who devised an ingenious way of determining atomic numbers by measuring the X rays given off by elements when they are used as targets in an X-ray tube. X rays, like ordinary light waves, can have a wide range of wavelengths. The wavelength is the distance between crests of a series of waves. And just as blue light has a shorter wavelength than red light, an X ray produced by one element can have a shorter wavelength than one produced by another element. Generally the shorter the wavelength, the more penetrating the X ray.

Working in 1913 and 1914, the years just before World War I, Moseley found that the wavelengths emitted by the elements decreased regularly when the elements were tested in the order in which they appear in the periodic table. Moseley was able to develop a mathematical relationship that correctly gave a correspondence between the wavelength of an X ray and the atomic number of the element. This relationship is today called Moseley's law.

Moseley used his law to find the correct atomic numbers for most of the elements. By arranging the elements in the periodic table according to their atomic number rather than by atomic weight, scientists discovered that many of the discrepancies they noted in the old arrangement disappeared.

The reason for the success of the new arrangement was that the chemical behavior of an element depends on the number of electrons it contains. Since atoms are electrically neutral, the atomic number also measures the number of electrons in an atom. The negative charges of the electrons must exactly balance the positive charges on the nucleus. As one moves across a row of the periodic table, the number of electrons as well as the atomic number is seen to increase. This discovery shed new light on the periodic table, implying some connection between an element's chemical properties and the number of electrons in its atom.

Henry Moseley developed a brilliant method for determining the correct atomic numbers for most of the elements.

Every element is now identified by its own unique atomic number. Hydrogen, for example, has an atomic number of 1 and has 1 electron. Helium has an atomic number of 2 and has 2 electrons. Sodium has an atomic number of 11, and has 11 electrons. The list of naturally found elements continues, up to uranium. Uranium has an atomic number of 92 and it has 92 electrons. (Two artificial elements have atomic numbers less than 92. So, although uranium is the largest of the 90 natural elements, it has an atomic number of 92.)

Moseley's brilliant career came to a tragic end in 1915 when he was only twenty-eight years old. After enlisting in the British army as a second lieutenant with the Royal Engineers, he was killed in action during the Gallipoli campaign in World War I.

ISOTOPES   In 1913 J. J. Thomson discovered that atoms with the same atomic number (and therefore the same number of electrons) can have slightly different masses. Such atoms are called isotopes of the same element. Working with a slightly modified form of the tube he originally used to discover the electron, he found that there were two kinds of neon atoms, neon-20 and neon-22. The numbers 20 and 22 are called the mass numbers of the atom, and refer to the approximate mass of the isotope rounded to the nearest whole number.

The mass of atoms is usually expressed in units called atomic mass units and abbreviated as amu. The unit is defined so that the mass of the hydrogen atom, the lightest atom, is about 1 amu. Thus the mass of neon-20 is about 20 amu.

The term *isotope* was first introduced in 1913 by Frederick Soddy, who was working with a group of seemingly different radioactive atoms that all had the same atomic number. He realized that they were all isotopes of the element thorium. The name *isotope* is derived from the Greek *iso*, meaning "same," and *topos*, meaning "place." Isotopes of a given element all occupy the same place in the periodic table because they have the same number of electrons and therefore are chemically similar.

Although isotopes are usually associated with radioactivity, almost every element has one or more stable isotopes. Hydrogen, for example, has three isotopes. Two of them, hydrogen-1 and hydrogen-2, are stable and both are found in nature. Hydrogen-2 is also known as deuterium, and when combined with oxygen forms "heavy" water. The third, hydrogen-3, is called tritium. Tritium is radioactive and is constantly being produced in the upper layers of the atmosphere. Rainwater contains a small amount of radioactive water formed from tritium, and this makes a small contribution to the natural background radiation we are all subject to. Most of the background radiation comes from such isotopes as carbon-14, potassium-90, and naturally occurring radioactive elements such as uranium and radon.

The isotopes of the elements whose atomic numbers are greater than about 80 are usually radioactive. Natural uranium, the heaviest of all the naturally occurring elements, is a mixture of two isotopes, and both are radioactive. The heavier one is called uranium-238 and constitutes about 99.3 percent of the uranium found in nature. The lighter one is called uranium-235 and makes up the remaining 0.7 percent.

THE PROTON   With the discovery of the nuclear atom, it became apparent that the nucleus of hydrogen, the smallest and lightest atom, was the simplest nucleus. Rutherford felt that it must play a special role as a building block of all other nuclei. Because of its importance, Rutherford chose to call it the proton, which comes from the Greek word *proteios*, meaning "of first importance."

The mass of the proton was determined by using such instruments as a mass spectrometer. With this instrument, a proton traveling at high speeds is injected into a magnetic field so that its path becomes bent in the form of a circle. By measuring the radius of this circle, scientists can arrive at the mass of a proton with great accuracy. The mass of the proton was measured and shown to be approximately 1 amu, or 1,836 times greater than the mass of the electron. The fact that a hydrogen atom is electrically neutral showed that the proton carries a single positive charge, exactly equal in magnitude to the charge on the electron.

By 1914 it was known that there were at least two basic particles, the electron and the proton. It seemed natural to assume therefore that heavier atoms were made up of two or more protons bound together in the nucleus, surrounded by the same number of electrons to make the atom electrically neutral. Rutherford seemed to confirm this in another of his famous alpha particle experiments. By now alpha particles had become synonymous with Rutherford, and scientists began to jokingly refer to alpha particles as Rutherford's "pets." In this experiment, he shot his positively charged projectiles at nitrogen, and observed that protons were ejected from the nitrogen nucleus. This certainly was consistent with the nitrogen nucleus being composed of protons.

But surprisingly, helium, the element following hydrogen in the periodic table, with an atomic number of 2 and with 2 electrons, has a mass four times that of a proton. Furthermore, lithium, the next element in the periodic table, with 3 electrons, has a mass seven times that of a proton. Where was the extra mass of the nucleus coming from?

THE NEUTRON   In a brilliant experiment performed in 1932, Sir James Chadwick (1891–1974), an English physicist, solved the case of the missing mass by discovering the neutron. He was awarded the Nobel Prize in physics in 1935 for his discovery. The neutron is a particle with a mass slightly greater than a proton, but without any electric charge.

Chadwick found the neutron by bombarding the metal beryllium with alpha particles. He noticed that some kind of neutral "radiation" was produced in the reaction. This radiation proved to have a powerful kick, since it could knock protons out of a hydrogen-containing sheet of white wax, commonly known as paraffin, that was placed in its path. It was like one billiard ball hitting another ball of the same mass, and sending it flying off across the table. Chadwick concluded that the neutral radiation must have a mass close to that of the proton, and announced the discovery of a new particle, the neutron.

The equipment Chadwick used for his work is small enough to be held in one's hand, and is still on display at the Cavendish Laboratory in Cambridge, England. Its size is all the more noteworthy when compared to the giant nuclear accelerators, some as long as several miles, now required to probe the atom.

Irène Curie (1897–1956), the daughter of Marie and Pierre Curie, and her husband, Frédéric Joliot-Curie (1900–1958), were also actively engaged in the hunt for the neutron, but narrowly missed discovering it. In 1933, however, they showed that materials could be made artificially radioactive by bombarding them with radiation. They shared the 1935 Nobel Prize in chemistry for this discovery. So the Curies, mother and daughter together with their husbands, won a total of five Nobel Prizes.

NUCLEAR STRUCTURE   The discovery of the neutron led to a more modern picture of the atom. Scientists now believed that there were three

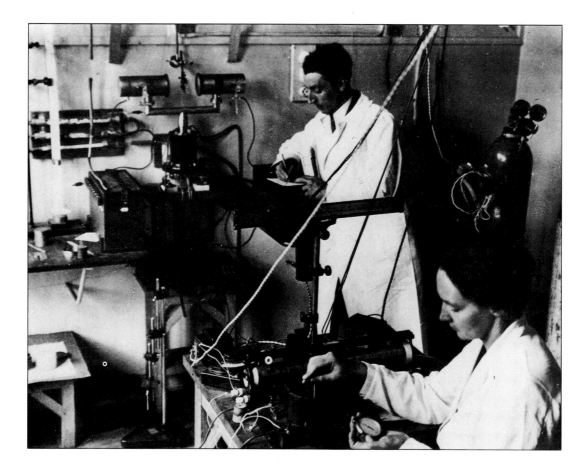

Irène and Frédéric Joliot-Curie discovered a way to make materials artificially radioactive.

types of subatomic particles: electrons, protons, and neutrons. Every atom was made up of a combination of these fundamental units. Protons and neutrons combined to form the nucleus of the atom, while the electrons were thought to move about the nucleus somewhat like planets about the Sun.

Since the proton has a positive charge, the number of protons in the nucleus determines the atomic number of the atom. With the exception of the lightest element, hydrogen, the nucleus of every other element contains neutrons in addition to its protons. We shall see that the neutrons, with no electric charge, contribute to the forces holding the nucleus together in the tiny core of the atom.

The nuclei of most of the smaller atoms have approximately the same number of neutrons as protons. In helium, for example, with an atomic number of 2, the nucleus contains 2 protons and 2 neutrons. The addition of 2 electrically neutral particles whose masses are about the same as the pro-

A traditional diagram of atomic structure, showing electrons orbiting around a central nucleus.

ton's mass explains the mystery of why helium contains 2 electrons but has a mass number of 4.

Similarly, the element lithium, with an atomic number of 3, has 3 electrons. The nucleus of lithium, however, contains 4 neutrons in addition to its 3 protons, which explains why lithium has a mass number of 7.

HOLDING TOGETHER   When we get to the larger atoms, which contain large numbers of protons, the mutual repulsion of the protons due to their positive charges becomes enormous. The number of neutrons in such atoms is always larger than the number of protons because neutrons are needed to contribute to the forces holding the nucleus together. A fairly big atom such as gold, for example, has an atomic number of 79, because it contains 79 protons, but it also contains 118 neutrons. Since both the proton and the neutron have a mass of approximately 1 amu, the mass number can be thought of as the total number of particles occupying the nucleus. Thus the mass number of the gold atom described above is 197, since 79 + 118 = 197.

With this model of the atom, the structure of isotopes can be easily explained. Isotopes of an element are simply atoms whose protons form nuclei with different numbers of neutrons. All the isotopes will therefore have the same atomic number but different mass numbers. Each of the three isotopes of hydrogen, for example, has one proton in its nucleus. But while the nucleus of hydrogen-1 contains no neutrons, the nucleus of deuterium has one neutron and that of tritium contains two neutrons.

It would be logical to assume that it should be possible to form an unlimited number of stable isotopes by adding neutrons. The more neutrons, the more nuclear contribution to cementing the nucleus together. A strange phenomenon begins to happen, however, when the number of neutrons gets too far out of balance with the number of protons. The atom becomes radioactive. This form of radioactivity is called beta decay, and it results in a neutron transforming itself into a proton. Even more surprising is that this change of identity is accompanied by the nucleus emitting an electron. (The original name for the electron was a beta particle, from which the process gets its name.)

If you see a person coming out of a house, you assume that the person was inside the house to start with. But electrons don't exist in the nucleus of an atom. So where does the emitted electron come from? And where does the nucleus get the energy to shoot out a fast-moving electron?

PLANETARY ELECTRONS   The planetary model of the nuclear atom in which electrons circle the nucleus is beautifully simple. It had to be abandoned, however, because it left many questions unanswered. According to a well-accepted and well-tested principle of physics, for example, a circling electron should quickly lose its energy, spiral into the nucleus, and immediately cause the atom to collapse. This doesn't happen. Why? Furthermore, if the small atomic world is really a replica of our solar system, how does the electron know what orbit to choose? Should it be close to the nucleus, or far out?

Then there is the question of the chemical behavior of the elements. The element argon has 18 electrons and is an inert gas. The next element in the periodic table is potassium, with 19 electrons. But potassium is a very reactive metal. Why should the addition of a single electron to an atom change its chemical properties so dramatically?

The answer to these questions, when it finally came, was based on revolutionary changes from the physics of the eighteenth and nineteenth centuries. A new kind of physics was called for, and it came in the form of quantum mechanics and the theory of relativity. These new ideas provided a window into the world of the atom.

FIVE

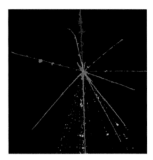

THE QUANTUM WORLD

WHAT IS LIGHT?   In many respects, "modern" physics began with studies on the nature of light. What is light? There have been many answers to this question during the past few hundred years, but by the nineteenth century it seemed clear that light was a wave.

It's easy to understand some of the properties of waves. Drop a stone in a lake and a circular pattern of waves will quickly spread over the surface of the water. If the wave passes a floating leaf, the leaf begins to bob up and down, so that we know the wave carries energy. You will remember that the distance between two wave crests is called the wavelength. The frequency of a wave is the number of times our floating leaf bobs up and down every second.

When water waves meet, they interfere with each other. The same is true of light waves. It was the English physicist Thomas Young's (1773–1829) interpretation of the interference of light that convinced most scientists that light was a wave. Young compared the interference between two rays of light to the interference of the waves produced by two stones dropped side by side into water. Each wave moves independently through the water. When the crest of one wave happens to coincide with the trough of another wave, they cancel each other out.

Exactly the same behavior is observed when two beams of light with the same wavelength illuminate a screen. When the crest of one light wave coincides with the trough of the other, they cancel each other out and produce darkness. When the crests of both waves happen to coincide, they add to each other, and a bright light is formed. What appears on the screen is a series of dark and light bands corresponding to one part of the screen receiving a great deal of light, and another part receiving no light at all. Only waves behave this way. Light, it was thought, was definitely a wave.

PARTICLES OF LIGHT   In 1905 Albert Einstein shocked the world of physics by proposing that light sometimes doesn't act like a wave, but behaves as if it were made up of a stream of particles. Each of these massless particles, or photons, as they were later called, is in effect a small package of energy. Einstein liked to say that each package carries a small "quantum" of energy. The amount of energy it carries depends on the kind of light we are dealing with. A photon of blue light, for example, has more energy than a photon of red light. The difference between blue light and red light, aside from our sensation of a color difference, is that the blue light has a greater frequency than the red.

Einstein expressed this dependence of photon energy on frequency in the celebrated equation: $E = hv$ where E is the quantum energy of the photon, v is the frequency of the light, and h is Planck's constant, which gives the proportional relation between quantum energy and frequency and is one of the most famous and important numbers in modern physics.

Planck's constant was named for the German physicist Max Karl Ernst Ludwig Planck (1858–1947), who investigated the relationship between the temperature of a hot object and the light it radiates. A red-hot poker, for example, will gradually become white when the temperature is increased. But no scientist was able to find a mathematical equation that would tell how intense the radiated color would be at a particular temperature.

Planck finally solved the problem in 1900 when he made his famous leap away from traditional physics, stating that for some reason a hot surface gives off light in little squirts or "packages" called quanta. He then found the constant h to express the energy of each of these little squirts of light. Planck later wrote of his discovery that "it was an act of desperation. I had to obtain a positive result, under any circumstances and at whatever cost." Planck was awarded the Nobel Prize in physics in 1918 for his discovery of energy quanta.

Einstein expanded on Planck's idea and made the even more radical conjecture that light itself, and not only the light given off by a hot surface, came in bundles of energy.

*Planck (left) and Einstein
(right) in a photograph
taken around 1929*

THE PHOTOELECTRIC EFFECT

With this new idea, Einstein was able to explain many aspects of the behavior of light in the photoelectric effect, behavior that had defied explanation by classical physics. In the photoelectric effect, light shining on a metal causes electrons to be given off by the metal. Photocells, which are devices that produce an electric current when light shines on them, work this way. They can be used, for example, to open the doors of a supermarket with a signal produced by the cell when someone blocks a beam of light.

The problem posed by the photoelectric effect, however, was that electrons come out of the metal only when the frequency of the light exceeds a certain value. Below this value, nothing happens, no matter how strong a light beam you use. Above this value, electrons are emitted even with the weakest possible light source. You might find, for example, that low-frequency red light produced by a superpowerful laser will not cause electrons to be emitted from a certain metal, but the high-frequency blue light given off by a firefly will.

To understand how puzzling this behavior is, imagine dropping a bottle off a pier into a lake and watching the ripples as they spread out from the splash. The ripples get smaller and smaller, and after a time are hardly visible. Suddenly, as the waves pass over another bottle floating in the lake a half mile away, that bottle is kicked out of the water by the impact. It is as though all the energy that originally was spread out over the waves suddenly concentrated itself into a small powerful particlelike projectile at the point of impact.

As you can see from the above example, trying to explain the photoelectric effect by using the wave theory of light leads to absurd results. Einstein boldly discarded the idea of waves as a carrier of light energy, and solved the riddle by substituting his idea that energy can only be absorbed from the light in quantum bundles of a certain definite size. He suggested that shining light on a metal meant shooting billions and billions of photons at the metal. When a photon hits an electron attached to an atom in the metal, it transfers all of its energy to the electron. This jolt knocks the electron loose from the atom and out of the metal. This can only happen, however, when the frequency of the light and therefore the energy of the photon is high enough to "liberate" the electron.

You might wonder why you can't see the "grainy" structure of light so that you're constantly observing flashes of light as photons hit your eye. The reason is that Planck's constant is so small. Expressed in the customary units used by physicists, it is a number approximately equal to 0.0000000 . . . 00063, with 33 zeros! Since the frequency of ordinary light is relatively low, a photon of green light, for example, has very little energy. Enormous numbers of photons are required to stimulate the eye, and the grainy character is overwhelmed by the sheer number of photons. The frequency of an X ray, however, is quite high, so that an individual X-ray photon is quite observable in its reaction, often harmful, with the atoms of a human cell.

The usefulness of Einstein's theory about the nature of light could not be denied, yet it faced opposition from many distinguished scientists for more than twenty years. Most found it unthinkable to give up the wave theory of light, which seemed to have been founded on unshakable observation and evidence. Finally, physicists began to realize that light had the properties of both light and particles. Young and Einstein were both right. The quantum world was proving to be stranger than anyone had imagined.

The concept of the light quantum won Einstein a Nobel Prize in physics in 1921. It also marked the birth of the quantum theory. By changing the rules of physics, the discovery of light particles, along with the quantum theory, led the way to a new understanding of the structure of the atom.

THE BOHR ATOM   In 1913 the Danish physicist Niels Bohr (1885–1962) published a paper on the structure of the hydrogen atom that made him famous almost overnight. He realized that the answer to the problem of the structure of the atom lay with the new quantum theory.

In Bohr's model of the hydrogen atom, a single electron circles around a nuclear proton like a planet about the Sun. But the strange feature of the electron motion is that it is only free to move in certain allowed orbits. Bohr called his orbits stationary states.

Rejecting the laws of the older, more traditional physics, Bohr made the startling assumption that as long as the electron remains in one of these orbits, the atom is stable, and no light is given off. Under ordinary circumstances the electron is found in the allowed orbit closest to the nucleus. This orbit is called the ground state. The electron must be given energy to jump up to an orbit higher than its ground state. Usually it quickly jumps down again. When the electron jumps down from one of its allowed orbits to one closer to the nucleus, however, it emits a photon whose energy is equal to the difference in energy between the two states.

To make his theory believable, Bohr had to somehow find a rule that determined which orbits were allowed and which were forbidden. Bohr intuitively felt that Planck's constant must again play a key role here, just as it did with Einstein's theory of the photon.

The concepts of physics usually have a dimension associated with them. A common dimension for distance, for example, is the mile, while speed can be expressed in miles per hour. Planck's constant also has a dimension, that of a concept called angular momentum. Bohr made the inspired assumption that it was the angular momentum of the electron, as it orbited the nucleus, that would determine the stationary states.

Bohr was the discoverer of electron orbitals.

Angular momentum is used in physics to describe the motion of rotating objects such as spinning balls or bicycle wheels. It involves not only how fast an object is spinning, but also its mass and shape. Very roughly, angular momentum measures how difficult it is to stop the object from spinning. The harder it is to stop it, the more angular momentum the spinning object has. It certainly is a lot easier to stop a spinning billiard ball than a huge mass like Earth, which is also a ball spinning once a day around its axis. The angular momentum of Earth is therefore much greater than that of the billiard ball.

What Bohr did was to make the radical suggestion that the angular momentum of the electron could only take certain values. The determining factor was Planck's constant h, the constant that seems to turn up everywhere in the world of the atom. Only those orbits were permitted whose angular momentum was $h/2\pi$, or two times $h/2\pi$, or three times $h/2\pi$, or some other integer times $h/2\pi$. (The symbol π, pronounced *pi* is the familiar ratio of the circumference to the diameter of a circle.)

There is a minimum angular momentum, namely $h/2\pi$, and this determines the closest orbit to the nucleus, the one the electron would occupy in normal hydrogen. Using this value, Bohr was able to calculate the size of the hydrogen atom. But Bohr's masterstroke was to account very accurately for the wavelengths of the light that hydrogen emits when it is heated and begins to glow.

SIX

WAVES OF MATTER

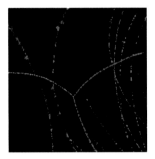

ATOMIC FINGERPRINTS   When sunlight passes through a prism, a beautiful spectrum of colors appears that seems to run continuously from red to blue. If you were to examine the light given off by a single element, however, like glowing neon, you would see only a few colored lines separated by dark spaces. These lines are called spectral lines. Each element has its unique set of colors, which can act like a fingerprint for the element. An astronomer, using a spectrograph, can take a photograph of the light given off by a star and then identify the elements present in the star by studying these lines.

You can see this yourself if you take a small amount of table salt in a spoon and hold it in the flame of a candle. As the salt burns, it gives off a fairly intense yellow light. This yellow light is the color of one of the spectral lines given off by sodium atoms, and is an important identifying color for the element. The sodium present in salt is, of course, part of the sodium chloride molecule.

The wavelengths of the colors in the spectral lines emitted when hydrogen is heated are very precisely known. Niels Bohr used his model of the atom to compute the wavelengths of light in this spectrum with great accuracy.

Bohr assumed that a photon was emitted by the atom whenever an electron jumped down from one of the atom's outer orbits ("excited" orbits, as he called them) to an orbit closer to the nucleus. The energy of the photon was equal to the difference in energy between the levels. Since only certain orbits were allowed, only photons of certain energies would be emitted.

Using Einstein's equation that relates the energy of a photon to its frequency, Bohr triumphantly calculated the frequencies corresponding to the colors observed in the hydrogen spectrum.

Bohr's work clarified what had been a confusing jumble of theories on the origin of spectral lines. The lines were clearly related to the changes in orbits of the electrons in an atom. The power of his theory amazed even Bohr, who late in life said, "Nobody thought one could get the basis of biology from the coloring of the wing of a butterfly." Bohr was awarded the Nobel Prize in physics in 1922 for his investigation of the structure of atoms.

Sunlight passing through a prism forms a spectrum of colors.

MATTER WAVES   With time it became clear that Bohr's model of the hydrogen atom had to be modified. Many attempts were made to apply his ideas to atoms more complicated than hydrogen, without success. The model could not explain the spectral lines given off by atoms with more than one electron, nor could it explain the influence of magnetic fields on the emitted light. A better theory was needed.

In 1923 Louis de Broglie (1892–1987), a member of an aristocratic French family, published a paper that has been described by other scientists as the Second French Revolution. Inspired by Einstein's particle-wave ideas, de Broglie suggested in a dissertation written as a requirement for a doctoral degree that, "Because photons have wave and particle characteristics, perhaps all forms of matter have wave as well as particle characteristics."

Within four years, there was convincing experimental evidence that de Broglie's idea was correct. There is now no doubt that electrons behave like waves, as do protons and neutrons. In fact, everything from teacups to bowling balls has a wave character. The effects of waves associated with a cup are not really observable because a cup is so large. But the effects of an electron wave can easily be seen.

A beam of electrons, for example, that is reflected from a polished metal surface shows the same variation in strong and weak intensity as a reflected beam of X rays. The only way to explain this is to assume that electrons have a wave character, since waves can reinforce each other in certain directions and cancel each other out in certain other directions.

Using these waves, de Broglie was able to justify Bohr's rule for the allowable electron orbits in hydrogen. If an electron behaves like a wave when it orbits the nucleus, it has to fit into an orbit in such a way as not to interfere with itself. This means that for a given wave, only certain orbits are permitted. The circumference of these allowed orbits is just the right length to prevent the crests of the electron waves from falling on the wave's troughs. Using an equation similar to one developed by Einstein for photons, de Broglie found the same orbits as those used by Bohr.

The wave theory was here to stay. De Broglie was awarded the Nobel Prize in physics in 1929 for his discovery of the wave nature of electrons.

But the model used by de Broglie still couldn't deal with atoms that had more than one electron or explain the effect of magnetic fields on atoms.

SPIN   In 1925 two young Dutch scientists, George Eugene Uhlenbeck (1900–1988) and Samuel Abraham Goudsmit (1902–1978), discovered that electrons spin on their own axes as well as revolve about the nucleus. Here again the analogy with a spinning Earth revolving about the Sun is very helpful in trying to visualize an atom. Today physicists rarely use this model, although it is helpful in explaining many of the properties of atoms.

There are two important consequences of electron spin. First of all, the

Louis de Broglie was the first to propose that matter has both wave and particle characteristics.

electron behaves like a little magnet since any moving electric charge always produces a magnetic field. The deflection of a compass held near a wire carrying electric current is an illustration of the magnetic field produced by electric charges, which are really electrons in motion. Secondly, because the electron is spinning it has a certain amount of angular momentum.

In the quantum world of the atom, Planck's constant, h, again plays an important role. The angular momentum associated with the spinning electron is always exactly $\frac{1}{2}$ times $h/2\pi$. Planck's constant is used so often that scientists usually say only that the electron has a spin of $\frac{1}{2}$.

And just as the electron is restricted to certain orbits in an atom, the spin of the electron has only two possible orientations, sometimes called spin "up" and spin "down." In trying to visualize the difference between the two spins, it is simplest to think of one orientation as clockwise and the other as counterclockwise.

The discovery of spin, with its two possible orientations, supplied one of the missing ingredients in quantum theory. It was now possible to account for the influence of magnetic fields on the spectral lines of different atoms. Of equal importance was the discovery that other particles have spin as well. Experiments showed that both the neutron and the proton also have a spin of ½, and strange as it may seem, even the photon, our light particle, has spin. The measured spin of the photon is 1, which means that its angular momentum is twice as great as that of an electron.

SEVEN

QUANTUM NUMBERS

*T*he Bohr theory of the atom, even with the de Broglie wave added, assumes that the electron orbits the nucleus in a definite circular pattern. This easy-to-visualize model needed still further refinement. It gave correct answers for hydrogen, but as before, it simply didn't work with atoms of more than one electron. A new theory had to be found, one that was based more profoundly on the wave character of electrons.

It was an Austrian physicist, Erwin Schrödinger (1887–1961), who used the wave picture of the electron in a consistent way to develop an equation that finally gave a firm foundation to the quantum theory of the atom. The Schrödinger equation, as it is called, is today the starting point for almost every problem involving atoms or molecules. Its applications range from the analysis of subatomic particles in giant accelerators to the behavior of giant biological molecules in our genes.

At the heart of Schrödinger's equation is the concept that the electron can be thought of as a "vibrating string." Using equations from traditional physics that described how waves behave under certain conditions, Schrödinger successfully created a quantum model that describes not only the hydrogen atom but also atoms that have more than one electron. Schrödinger was awarded the Nobel Prize in physics in 1933 for the discovery of new productive forms of atomic theory.

In Schrödinger's model, there is no longer any such thing as a well-defined electron orbit. Schrödinger dealt only with the probability of finding the electron in a certain place about the nucleus. In place of orbits,

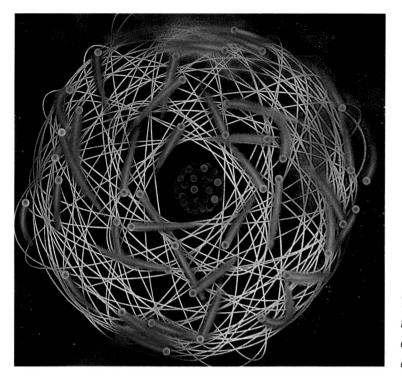

*This is an artist's concep-
tion of a nucleus surrounded by a cloud of orbiting
electrons.*

physicists now speak of "electron clouds." These are not clouds, of course, only fuzzy pictures that resemble the superimposition of hundreds of snapshots of the position of the electron over a period of time. For some electrons in an atom, these clouds are spherical, while for others they might be oval shaped. These figures are wave patterns of electrons confined to existing in the region around the nucleus of an atom.

The solutions of the Schrödinger equation are usually expressed in terms of probabilities. We can get an approximate idea of how electron wave patterns are determined by looking at a set of numbers called quantum numbers. Quantum numbers are part of the solution of the Schrödinger equation.

The electron spin is an example of a quantum number. It is usually identified by the letter s. We have seen that the spin quantum number of an electron is $1/2$. In effect the electron behaves as if it were a ball of spinning charge and its quantum number defines its angular momentum as it spins. The spin can be either clockwise or counterclockwise.

Three more quantum numbers are applied to atomic electrons, each describing some restriction on their motion. The first of these, represented by the letter n, defines the size of an orbital wave about the nucleus. It is

*E*rwin Schrödinger, creator of an equation that is the starting point for most problems involving atoms or molecules

called the principal quantum number because it determines the energy of an atom.

Another quantum number, represented by the letter *l*, specifies the angular momentum of an electron as it revolves about the nucleus. Remember that the electron not only spins on its own axis but also revolves about the nucleus like Earth revolves about the Sun. This quantum number specifies the shape of the electron wave patterns.

Finally, a quantum number called *m* is used to express the orientation or tilt of the electron waves with respect to each other.

These four quantum numbers, *s*, *n*, *l*, and *m*, determine the wave pattern of the electron about the nucleus. The wave pattern tells us where the electron has a good chance of being found if we try to locate it in an experiment.

The wave patterns of electrons determine how atoms fit together when they

> **QUANTUM NUMBERS**
>
> *s* = electron spin; can be clockwise or counterclockwise
>
> *n* = size of the orbital wave. The principal quantum number, it determines the energy of an atom.
>
> *l* = angular momentum of an electron as it revolves about the nucleus; specifies the shape of the electron wave patterns
>
> *m* = tilt of electron waves with respect to each other

form molecules. All the symmetries and beautiful patterns we see around us in snowflakes or crystals or flowers are the result of wave patterns in atoms.

THE EXCLUSION PRINCIPLE

More questions needed to be answered. What determines how the electrons arrange themselves around the nucleus of an atom? This, after all, determines the chemical behavior of the atom. And why do elements right next to each other in the periodic table, like sodium and neon, behave so differently? As explained earlier, neon is a nonreactive gas, while sodium, with only one more electron, is a metal reactive enough to burst into flames when exposed to air.

These questions were solved by Wolfgang Pauli (1900–1958), the brilliant Austrian-born physicist whose article on Einstein's theory of relativity made him famous at the age of twenty-one. While investigating the spectral lines given off by atoms, he made a spectacular discovery that has proven indispensable in understanding why atoms have different chemical properties.

Pauli's solution is called the exclusion principle. It states that "in an atom there can never be two or more electrons with the same four quantum

Wolfgang Pauli's discovery of the exclusion principle solved the mystery of why atoms have different chemical properties.

numbers." In other words, no two electrons in an atom can be in the same quantum "place" at the same time. This means that each electron must have a different wave pattern.

The electrons in a large atom occupy a series of atomic orbitals called shells. Each of these shells has a different quantum number n, and therefore a different energy. Some electrons must occupy higher energy shells because the lower energy shells are already filled.

A helium atom, for example, has two electrons. Although these electrons have identical values of the n, l, and m quantum numbers, they must have different values of the spin quantum number, s. One electron spins clockwise and the other counterclockwise. They both can therefore occupy the same shell, with $n = 1$. Lithium, the next element in the periodic table, has three electrons. The third electron has no place to go but to a new quantum shell, one defined by the quantum number $n = 2$. This shell is farther from the nucleus and therefore has a higher energy.

The same pattern repeats itself as we continue to atoms with higher atomic numbers. Electrons fill lower energy shells until they are fully occupied, and then start filling the next higher energy shell. It is the wave pattern of the last electron added that often determines the properties of an atom. The addition of an electron to atoms that have a complete shell, such as neon and argon, can therefore completely change the way the atoms behave.

The columns of the periodic table, which correspond to elements with similar chemical behavior, contain elements with the same number of electrons in the outermost shell. These outer electrons are usually called valence electrons.

As you go across a row in the periodic table, that outermost shell is being filled. The chemical behavior of the elements repeats periodically because electron wave patterns about the nucleus periodically repeat as shells of an atom are filled. In other words, an atom with one electron outside two filled shells behaves very much like an atom with one electron outside three filled shells.

Pauli was awarded the Nobel Prize in physics in 1945 for the discovery of the exclusion principle.

EIGHT

THE PARTICLE EXPLOSION

Until the early 1930s, the atom was thought to be made up only of protons, neutrons, and electrons. These particles seemed to be the fundamental building blocks of all atoms. And, as in the old idea of the atom, they were considered indivisible. More challenges and surprises were to come, however. As scientists began to develop the tools to probe more deeply into the subatomic world, they discovered new and totally unexpected phenomena.

SPECIAL THEORY OF RELATIVITY   The subatomic world proved to be one where particles were constantly being created and destroyed. Einstein's theory of relativity, first published in 1905, was an essential guide through this world.

The theory of relativity is certainly one of the most famous of the twentieth century. It immediately conjures up thoughts of space travel and atomic bombs. Roughly speaking, it springs from the very simple idea that the laws of physics are the same in all frames of reference.

At first glance, this idea doesn't seem remarkable. But it took an Einstein to follow this one thought through to its logical conclusions. One of these conclusions was the discovery of the equivalence of mass and energy. Under the proper conditions, matter can be changed into energy and energy can be changed into matter.

The exact relationship between energy and matter is given in Einstein's celebrated equation $E = mc^2$. Here E is the energy, m stands for the mass, and c for the speed of light. Since the speed of light is so great (186,000 miles or 300,000 kilometers per second), the equation also tells us that the amount of energy equivalent to a small amount of mass is enormous. Converting 1 gram of matter into energy over a period of one day, for example, would generate enough electric power to light a small city!

As we explore the nucleus of an atom, strange new particles constantly appear and disappear. The ability of energy to transform itself into matter is the key to understanding these changes.

THE STRONG FORCE   The nucleus of most atoms contains many positively charged protons squeezed together in a small space. Since positively charged particles repel each other, the nucleus should fly apart, and atoms as we know them should cease to exist. Evidently there must be another force in the nucleus, a force powerful enough to overcome the disruptive effects of electrical repulsion. Physicists simply called it the strong force, the name by which it is still known.

Why did it take so long to realize that a strong force exists? We certainly are aware of the force of gravity. If we drop a book, or try to jump, or throw a ball, the effect of gravity is very apparent. Electric forces are equally important in our everyday life, although they are not so obvious and are often not identified as such. Every time you touch something, or feel the wind in your face, or flex a muscle, it is the electric force you are experiencing. But, even though it's about one hundred times stronger than the electric force, the strong force is hard to observe.

This is because the strong force has a very short range. The range of a force is like the length of a boxer's arm—stand a little beyond it, and even if he throws his best punch, you feel nothing. Unlike gravity and the electric force, which can act over huge intergalactic distances, the strong force simply disappears at distances greater than the size of an average nucleus.

The strong force is an attractive force that binds neutrons and protons together. We shall see later that the strong force really acts between quarks, particles even smaller than neutrons or protons. Quarks are the basic building blocks of neutrons and protons.

THE CASE OF THE MISSING ENERGY   Another puzzle facing physicists was the radioactivity of certain atoms. Particularly intriguing was a form of radioactivity called beta decay. We have already noted that during beta decay, a neutron in the nucleus of the radioactive atom changes itself into a proton. This increases the atomic number of the atom by 1, and changes it into a new element. The radioactive atom also emits an electron (beta particle) as part of the process. We know that electrons don't exist in the nucleus, yet here is an electron leaving a nucleus. The only possible explanation is that the electron is first created and then emitted during the process.

An example of an atom that undergoes beta decay is carbon-14. This radioactive isotope of carbon is used for dating ancient objects such as manuscripts and samples of wood, charcoal, and bone. Using carbon dating, for example, samples of wood and bone have been identified as having existed from 1,000 to 20,000 years ago.

As a result of beta decay, the carbon emits an electron and transforms itself into nitrogen. The carbon's atomic number has increased by 1, since a new proton has been formed in the nucleus. The electron that is emitted from the nucleus has a great deal of energy. In fact, much of the damage caused by radioactive atoms is due to these fast-moving electron "bullets," which can penetrate our bodies and damage cells.

What was particularly intriguing about beta decay in general was that it seemed to violate two very basic and important principles of physics. One was the conservation of energy. This principle states that the total energy of the system in a reaction of this kind always remains the same. It can change its form, as when the energy you use rubbing your hand on a table is transformed into heat, but it is still there. With beta decay, some energy appeared to be "missing."

In beta decay, the available energy is calculated using the difference in mass of the nucleus before it decays and after. The lost mass has been converted into the energy of the emitted electron. This energy was found to range from near zero to the full amount of energy equivalent to the lost mass. The "energy books" didn't balance.

Another puzzle was that the angular momentum of the reaction didn't add up correctly. One spin-½ particle, a neutron, decayed into two spin-½ particles, a proton and an electron. This seemed to violate the physical principle that angular momentum, like energy, is conserved.

The reason you can ride your bike without falling is that the angular momentum of the spinning wheels does not want to change. It is this resistance to change that keeps you from falling over on a moving bicycle. The same tendency for the angular momentum not to change will cause skaters spinning slowly on ice with outstretched arms to suddenly increase the speed of their spin dramatically when they pull in their arms.

THE NEUTRINO

The mystery of the missing energy and spin was solved by Wolfgang Pauli in 1931. In a famous letter to other scientists, he made the simple-sounding suggestion that along with the electron, another particle, one that nobody had ever seen, is also emitted during beta decay. This silent accomplice, called a neutrino, carries off the missing energy. The conservation of energy is not violated after all.

Pauli also guessed that the neutrino had a spin of $\frac{1}{2}$, the same spin as protons and electrons. This would balance the angular momentum correctly and be consistent with another conservation law of physics.

Pauli guessed correctly both times. After searching for twenty years, a team of "particle hunters" finally observed the neutrino. It was well known that enormous numbers of beta decay reactions occur in a nuclear reactor as a by-product of fission. In 1956, using a nuclear reactor near Savannah, Georgia, as a source of neutrinos, two American physicists, Clyde Lorrain Cowan (1919–1974) and Frederick Reines (1913–), performed an ingenious experiment that finally provided confirmation of the neutrino's existence.

The name *neutrino* means "little neutral one" in Italian. The particle owes its name to the fact that it has no electric charge, and little or no mass. Perhaps the neutrino's most extraordinary property is that it interacts so weakly with matter. Hundreds of billions of neutrinos given off by the Sun pass through your body every second without doing any damage. They can also pass right through Earth without being stopped.

THE WEAK FORCE

Pauli's prediction of the existence of the neutrino led the great Italian nuclear physicist Enrico Fermi (1901–1954) to publish a paper on the theory of beta decay in 1934. In his theory, Fermi makes use of a new nuclear force, one that is capable of changing a neutron into a proton accompanied by an electron and a neutrino. He reasoned that if a nucleus can create and emit a photon during beta decay, then it also can create an electron and a neutrino, if enough energy is available. This new force was eventually named the weak force to distinguish it from the strong nuclear force.

The weak force is indeed about ten million times weaker than the strong force. Its range is even shorter than that of the strong force, operat-

*E*nrico Fermi used
neutrons to create new
nuclear reactions.

ing over distances that are about one-hundredth the size of a proton.
Although this force is weak, it is important for reactions where the strong
force or the electric force does not operate. The best example of this is the
creation and reactions of neutrinos. Fermi won the Nobel Prize in physics in
1938 for work in quite a different area of physics. He was honored for his
discovery of nuclear reactions that were brought about by neutrons.

FORCE CARRIERS   It is easy to imagine a force when you push a table
across a room. Your hand is in contact with the table, and you can feel the
table's resistance as it moves. But the electric force and gravity are more
mysterious. They seem to act at a distance, without any apparent contact.

How can Earth be attracted to the Sun, for example, when the two objects are separated by millions of miles of empty space? And how can a positively charged proton attract a negatively charged electron in an atom, when they are separated by a vacuum?

In modern quantum theory, forces are transmitted to a distant object by the exchange of particles. It's rather like two children who interact by throwing snowballs at each other. The snowballs can be thought of as a kind of messenger that tells the children to either come closer or to move farther apart.

Each of the four forces—gravity, the electric force, the strong force, and the weak force—has its own exchange particle, which acts as a carrier of the force. The carrier of gravity is a particle called a graviton, but it has never been observed in any experiment. On the other hand, the carrier of the electric force is the photon, which you see every time you turn on a lamp. When an electron repels another electron, the two particles are constantly exchanging short-lived photons with each other.

The carrier of the strong force is called a gluon. Not many physicists believed in its existence at first. There was a dramatic change in attitude, however, when experimental evidence for its existence began to accumulate.

The gluon is the particle that "glues" neutrons and protons together and prevents the nucleus from disintegrating. We have already mentioned that neutrons and protons are themselves made up of other particles called quarks. It is more accurate therefore to think of gluons being exchanged between quarks.

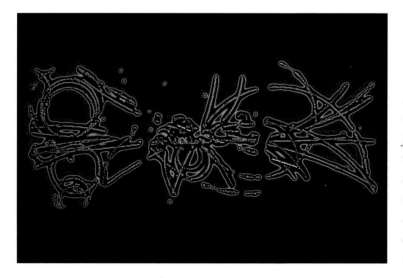

A false-color version of the original image obtained from a particle detector when the Z particle was discovered. The particle itself lives too briefly to be seen. Its existence is deduced from other information in the image.

The carriers of the weak force are known as the $W+$, the $W-$, and the $Z°$ particles. Unlike the other exchange particles, which have no mass, the weak force exchanges particles that have a huge mass. Their masses are approximately one hundred times the mass of a proton. Their discovery and identification represented a major triumph for the high-energy experimental physics

THE FOUR FORCES

FORCE	EXCHANGE PARTICLE	MASS
gravity	graviton (particle has not been directly observed)	none
electric	photon	none
strong	gluon	none
weak	$W+$, $W-$, and $Z°$ (intermediate vector bosons)	huge

community of scientists and their accelerators. The force carriers for the weak force have come to be called intermediate vector bosons.

ANTIPARTICLES   In February 1928 the English physicist Paul Adrien Maurice Dirac (1902–1984), one of the major contributors to the early development of quantum mechanics, announced his discovery of an equation that combined Einstein's theory of relativity and quantum mechanics.

One of the consequences of Dirac's work was the startling prediction that a new kind of electron should exist, one with a positive charge. This positive electron, which later came to be called a positron, is an example of an antiparticle. It is identical to an ordinary electron in every respect except for its charge. Dirac's prediction turned into a triumph when Carl David Anderson (1905–1991) accidentally collected experimental evidence of the positron in 1932 while investigating tracks produced by cosmic ray particles in a cloud chamber. Dirac shared the Nobel Prize in physics with Erwin Schrödinger in 1933 for his work in atomic theory. Carl Anderson was awarded the Nobel Prize in physics in 1936, sharing the prize with Victor Franz Hess, the discoverer of cosmic rays.

Cosmic ray particles have been a crucial part of many of the discoveries of modern physics. In a way, they serve as a cost-free nuclear accelerator in the sky. Cosmic rays are, to a large extent, protons that arrive at Earth from outer space with tremendous amounts of energy. They strike the atoms in the upper layers of Earth's atmosphere to produce many kinds of nuclear reactions.

The positrons that Anderson observed were created from energy in the form of photons produced by cosmic rays. In a reaction known as pair pro-

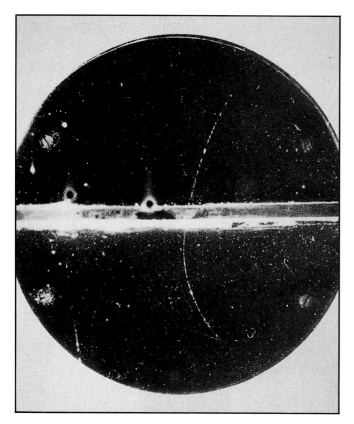

The discovery photograph of the positron, the first antiparticle to be discovered

duction, a photon changes itself into an electron and a positron. There must be enough energy available to make that much mass, of course, and this is always determined by Einstein's equation $E = m\mathrm{c}^2$.

With enough energy, heavier pairs of particles and antiparticles can be made. The antiproton was discovered in 1955, by scientists using a proton accelerator called the Bevatron located at the University of California at Berkeley. This was the beginning of "big science," where experiments were done with huge machines and large teams of scientists working on a single experiment. The two leaders of the Berkeley team, Owen Chamberlain (1920–) and Emilio G. Segrè (1905–1989), were awarded the Nobel Prize in physics in 1959 for the discovery of the antiproton. The antineutron was discovered there a year later.

The Bevatron is capable of producing billions of electron volts of energy, which means that a particle, such as an electron, has an energy it would acquire if it were accelerated through one billion volts. Such enormous energy is needed to create antiparticles that have approximately 2,000 times more mass than an electron.

Owen Chamberlain, one of the
discoverers of the antiproton

We now know that every particle has an antiparticle. Even neutral particles, such as neutrons and neutrinos, have antiparticles. Some particles, like
the photon, are their own antiparticle. Almost all the antiparticles have to be
artificially created in high-energy laboratories. When particles and antiparticles collide, they destroy each other on contact. Physicists like to say they
"annihilate" each other. This is the reverse of the process of making a
positron. The particles disappear, and energy, usually in the form of photons, is created.

Why our universe is made of matter but contains no antimatter is still
an open question. Some scientists believe that during the early history of the
universe there were equal amounts of matter and antimatter. Then for some
unknown reason, the antimatter vanished. Scientists once thought that some
distant galaxies might be made of antimatter, but we now know that this is
not so.

Some scientists believe that the absence of antimatter in the universe is
due to some unknown fluctuation or force that caused more matter than
antimatter to exist in the original creation of matter. And once most of the

matter and antimatter had annihilated each other, all that was left was the leftover matter. Other scientists think that part of the explanation of the disappearance of antimatter is that it has such a dangerous existence here on Earth since it annihilates on contact with matter.

Modern experimental physics is constantly creating new particles by first creating high-energy photons through the annihilation of other particles. Particles and antiparticles, for example, are routinely created in laboratories today. Large accelerators collide beams of electrons and positrons to produce enormous bursts of energy in the form of photons that physicists call annihilation photons. These photons, in turn, create pairs of new particles, almost like matter condensing out from the newly formed energy.

NEW PARTICLES AND THE STRONG FORCE   In 1934 the Japanese physicist Hideki Yukawa (1907–1981) proposed the existence of a new particle as part of his theory of the strong force. Since the strong force has a short range, he reasoned that the particle would have a fairly large mass. This follows from a principle of quantum mechanics known as the Heisenberg uncertainty principle. Named for one of the creators of quantum mechanics, Werner Karl Heisenberg (1901–1976), it predicts that the shorter the range of a force, the more massive its exchange particle. In the language of Heisenberg, this is roughly equivalent to saying, the greater the mass of the exchange particle, the greater the energy that must be borrowed to create the particle, and the briefer the time the particle exists before the energy must be returned.

It was a brilliant conjecture on the part of Yukawa, since no one had ever seen this particle. By estimating its range, he calculated the mass to be about one-seventh the mass of a proton but about 200 to 300 times the mass of an electron. He also predicted that this particle would come in three different forms, one positively charged, one negatively charged, and one electrically neutral.

Yukawa's charged particles, which today are called pions, were found in 1947 by Cecil Frank Powell (1903–1969) at Bristol University in England. These pions were found in the cosmic rays showering down onto Earth. To detect them, Powell and his team had to trek to the Bolivian Andes and set up their measuring equipment at an elevation of 18,000 feet (5,500 meters) above sea level. Yukawa was awarded the Nobel Prize in physics in 1949 for his prediction of a new particle based on theoretical work on nuclear forces. Powell was awarded the Nobel Prize in physics the next year.

Some ten years earlier, teams of scientists investigating cosmic rays at sea level claimed to have discovered particles similar to the particle described by Yukawa. These particles were "impostors," however, and were actually the product of the decay of the true Yukawa pion. The pion is unstable and decays after about one-hundredth of a millionth of a second, long before it can reach sea level.

These impostor particles, with a mass of one-ninth rather than the predicted one-seventh the mass of a proton, are called muons. Muons have nothing to do with the strong interaction, and were and still are rather mysterious. Even the muon's discoverer, Powell, admitted that "we know what muons are, but we don't know what they are for in the grand design of things."

Except for the fact that they are unstable, decaying after about one-millionth of a second into electrons and neutrinos, muons behave in most respects like heavy electrons. And except for their mass, they look just like electrons. Some physicists call them fat electrons.

Yukawa's pions exist, but they turned out not to be the true carrier of the strong force. Gluons are. The charged pions live for a short period of time and then decay into muons and neutrinos.

After many years of the study of pion decays, it became apparent that the neutrino created along with the muon is different from the electron neutrino described by Wolfgang Pauli. The critical experiment confirming that the neutrinos were different was performed in 1961 by a group of physicists led by Leon M. Lederman (1922–), Melvyn Schwartz (1932–), and Jack Steinberger (1921–). Using the large Alternating Gradient Synchrocyclotron accelerator at Brookhaven National Laboratory in Upton, on Long Island, New York, they produced an intense beam of pions that decayed to produce muon neutrinos. These neutrinos interacted with matter in such a manner as to indicate that they were quite different from electron neutrinos. Lederman, Schwartz, and Steinberger shared the 1989 Nobel Prize in physics for this discovery. A recent discovery of yet another neutrino, different from the electron and muon neutrinos, indicates that there are actually three different kinds of neutrinos.

The neutrino is an extremely elusive particle, and massive efforts are needed to detect it. One such detector, for example, used to detect neutrinos

*P*art of the enormous neutrino detector at the Brookhaven National Laboratory

arriving at Earth from outer space, consists of an enormous tank of cleaning fluid located deep underground at the Homestead Gold Mine in South Dakota. Another is located in an abandoned salt mine in Ohio, approximately 2,000 feet (3,200 meters) below the surface of the earth, and consists of an enormous tank of pure water. Every so often, a neutrino passes through the earth and collides with an electron or a proton in the water, creating a new charged particle. In turn, the newly created particle will produce a flash of light that is detected by special light sensors called photomultiplier tubes lining the walls of the tank.

STRANGE PARTICLES   During the 1950s and 1960s, an incredible variety of new subatomic particles were discovered. After the success of Powell and his team at high altitudes, mountain climbing became very popular for physicists looking for something new in cosmic rays.

Many of these efforts were successful. A new particle called the kaon was discovered that behaved in many respects like a heavy pion. Another group of physicists discovered a massive particle they called a lambda particle. As large accelerators joined in the search, the trickle of new particles turned into a flood. Hundreds of new particles were found. They came to be known collectively as strange particles, and physicists jokingly talked about the "particle zoo."

Things became so confused that Willis E. Lamb (1913–), who shared the 1955 Nobel Prize in physics with Polykarp Kusch, suggested that "the finder of a new elementary particle used to be rewarded by a Nobel Prize, but such a discovery ought now to be punished by a $10,000 fine."

The discovery of quarks would finally put some order into the chaos of particle physics.

NINE

THE STANDARD MODEL

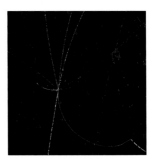

The state of physics in the early 1960s reminded many scientists of the disorder in chemistry before the elements were organized into the periodic table. Like the chemists of that earlier time, physicists began to organize and classify the long list of particles that had been discovered. Underlying this attempt to restore order was the belief that some fundamentally simple principle lay behind the apparent complexity of the universe.

An early attempt to classify particles according to their weight didn't work very well. A middleweight particle like the muon, for example, had more in common with a light particle like the electron than with another middleweight particle like the pion. (The Particle Tree on page 79 may make this chapter easier to understand and remember.)

FERMIONS AND BOSONS   At first, physicists looking for common features to classify particles found that differences in spin helped them to create some order in the general clutter. To help them understand how particles behave when clustered together in atoms and nuclei, they created two broad groups, called fermions and bosons. Fermions, named in honor of Enrico Fermi, are particles with half-integer spins, like the proton, neutron, and electron. Bosons are particles with spin equal to zero or with whole-integer spins, like the photon and the pion. Bosons are named in honor of the Indian physicist Satyendranath Bose (1894–1974).

An important distinction between the two groups is that fermions are subject to the Pauli exclusion principle, while bosons are not. Physicists could immediately deduce from this that no two electrons, being fermions, could occupy the same quantum state. This was the important principle that showed how electrons fill energy shells in an atom.

HADRONS AND LEPTONS   As useful as the spin is in predicting certain types of behavior, it still left too many questions unanswered. Both the proton and the electron are spin-$\frac{1}{2}$ fermions, yet a proton attracts a neutron, while the electron is immune to this strong interaction. Since physicists were interested in how particles interact, the principle they finally selected to classify them was whether or not the particle was sensitive to the strong force.

Therefore yet two more broad families of particles were created. Those sensitive to the strong force were called hadrons (from the Greek *adros*, meaning "strong") and those immune to it were called leptons (from the Greek *leptos*, meaning "small").

The family of leptons consists of 6 particles. It includes the electron, the muon, and the recently discovered tau particle. Each of these particles has a different neutrino associated with it. The tau particle, discovered in 1975, came as a great surprise because it was so massive. It has a mass twice that of a proton. The leptons share two other important properties: they are all fermions, and they seem to have no internal structure. In that sense, they are true fundamental particles.

The hadrons contain both fermions and bosons. Protons, neutrons, pions, and antiprotons are all examples of hadrons. Unlike the relatively few leptons that have been observed—there are only six of them—there seems to be no end to the number of hadrons. Several hundred have been seen in laboratories throughout the world, with no end in sight.

We now know that the reason for this striking number of hadrons is that hadrons are really composite particles, made up of more fundamental particles called quarks.

Physicists found it convenient to split hadrons into two smaller families. The fermions were separated from the bosons. Hadrons that are fermions are called baryons (from the Greek word *barys*, meaning "heavy") and hadrons that are bosons are called mesons (from the Greek word *meso*, meaning "middle").

The table on the next page clarifies these categories for some of the particles we have discussed. The spin of each particle is shown next to its name.

LEPTONS	HADRONS	
	Baryons	**Mesons**
(Fermions)	(Fermions)	(Bosons)
electron ($1/2$)	neutron ($1/2$)	pion (0)
electron neutrino ($1/2$)	proton ($1/2$)	kaon (0)
muon ($1/2$)	lambda particle ($1/2$)	
muon neutrino ($1/2$)		
tau neutrino ($1/2$)		
tau particle ($1/2$)		

THE EIGHTFOLD WAY   The two large families of hadrons kept growing. When the accelerator known as the Cosmotron started operating in 1952 at the Brookhaven National Laboratory in Upton, New York, it began producing a flood of unexpected "strange" particles. New heavy mesons and baryons made their appearance in the laboratory. To explain the observed behavior of these particles, Murray Gell-Mann (1929–) at the California Institute of Technology in Pasadena invented a "strangeness" number that seemed to "explain" why certain reactions occur and others don't. He assigned a number to each hadron and found that the total strangeness of the hadrons during a strong interaction remained constant. The numbers were quite arbitrary, however, and physicists still sensed that chaos reigned.

Murray Gell-Mann introduced a measure of order into atomic science in 1961, when he introduced the Eightfold Way. (The same idea was suggested independently by the Israeli physicist Yuval Ne'eman (1925–), a member of Israeli Defense who was studying physics in London.) Gell-Mann took this name from a passage in Buddhist scripture.

Gell-Mann and Ne'eman found that it was possible to arrange families of baryons and mesons into beautiful symmetric hexagonal and triangular geometric shapes, according to some of their common properties, such as charge and spin. The family of mesons with zero spin, for example, forms a striking hexagonal pattern with one particle at each vertex and two particles in the center. Some of these patterns have lovely snowflakelike forms.

The most impressive result of Gell-Mann and Ne'eman's work was the ability to use vacancies in these patterns to predict the properties of particles that had not as yet been discovered. Perhaps the most spectacular success

*M*urray Gell-Mann, one of the most
creative thinkers of modern physics

was finding the omega minus particle. The creators of the Eightfold Way
had organized a family of ten particles into a pyramidal shape. No one had
found evidence of the particle that should have occupied the apex of the
pyramid, but Gell-Mann used his model to predict its characteristics. He
called it omega minus because it should have a negative charge, and because
it would be the last particle in the pyramid to be found. Omega is the last
letter of the Greek alphabet. Gell-Mann was awarded the Nobel Prize in
physics in 1969 for his contributions and discoveries concerning the classifi-
cation of elementary particles.

Any doubts that these geometric patterns were more than a coincidence
vanished when the omega minus particle was discovered in 1964 at
Brookhaven National Laboratory. It was a great victory for the Eightfold
Way. The prediction of the existence of the omega minus particle has often
been compared to Mendeléev's predicting the properties of the missing elements in his periodic table.

QUARKS   Despite its success, the Eightfold Way could not explain why
hadrons fit into these curious patterns. Hidden in the patterns, however, was
the suggestion that perhaps baryons and mesons are, after all, made up of a
small number of fundamental building blocks.

A particle physicist studies a computer display of a particle collision at CERN.

The breakthrough came in 1964 when Gell-Mann and George Zweig (1937–), a scientist working at the Center for European Nuclear Research (CERN) laboratory in Geneva, Switzerland, independently proposed that all hadrons are made up of more elementary particles. Gell-Mann called these particles quarks, a name borrowed from a passage in *Finnegans Wake*, a novel by James Joyce. In keeping with his somewhat eccentric choice of names, Gell-Mann always liked to remind students that *quark* rhymes with *fork* and not with *bark*.

In Gell-Mann's original work, there were three types of quarks, called flavors by physicists: an "up" quark, a "down" quark, and a "strange" quark. Each quark had an antiquark. Perhaps the most extraordinary feature of these quarks was that, contrary to any previously observed particles, they had fractional charges. The simplified table below shows the assigned charges:

QUARK FLAVORS	CHARGES
up	$+2/3$
antiup	$-2/3$
down	$-1/3$
antidown	$+1/3$
strange	$-1/3$
antistrange	$+1/3$

The quark model claimed that every hadron could be built up from combinations of quarks. The rules of the game were:

Every baryon is made up of three quarks.
Every antibaryon is made up of three antiquarks.
Every meson is made up of a quark and an antiquark.

In this model, a proton, for example, is made up of three quarks, two up quarks and a down quark. The charges on the quarks add up to +1, which is

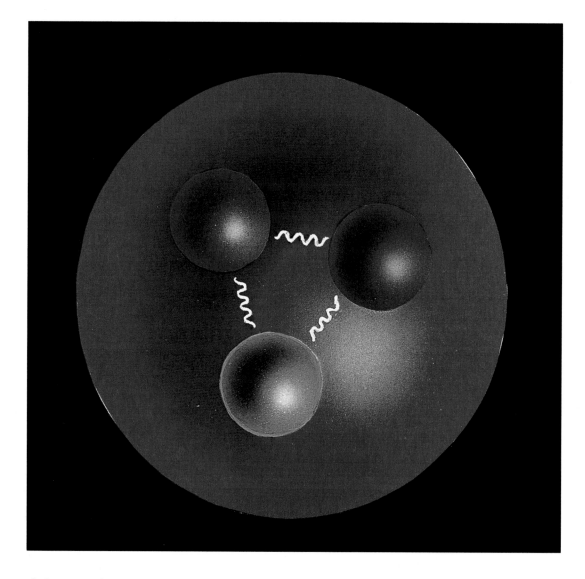

A *diagram of the structure of the proton. A proton consists of three quarks, bound together by the strong force. Two of the quarks are "up" quarks and one is a "down" quark.*

consistent with the charge on the proton. A neutron consists of an up quark and two down quarks, which add up to a zero charge.

DO QUARKS EXIST?

The success of the model is astonishing. Every hadron known in 1960 could be accounted for. The one thing that prevented the quark model from being universally accepted was that in spite of the most strenuous search over a period of thirty years, no one has ever seen a free quark. If a proton is really made of three quarks, it should be possible to knock one of them out of a proton by hitting the proton hard enough. This has never been achieved.

> *Proton = 3 quarks*
>
> $2 \text{ up} = 2 \times +\tfrac{2}{3} = +\tfrac{4}{3}$
> $+1 \text{ down} = 1 \times -\tfrac{1}{3} = -\tfrac{1}{3}$
> _____
> $+\tfrac{3}{3} = 1$

> *Neutron = 3 quarks*
>
> $1 \text{ up} = 1 \times +\tfrac{2}{3} = +\tfrac{2}{3}$
> $+2 \text{ down} = 2 \times -\tfrac{1}{3} = -\tfrac{2}{3}$
> _____
> 0

How, then, do we know that quarks really exist? Physicists can probe the interior of a proton using the same technique used by Ernest Rutherford decades earlier to establish the nuclear atom. Experiments done in 1967 at the two-mile-long Stanford Linear Accelerator (SLAC), located at Stanford University in California, fired electrons at protons and observed how they scattered. As was the case with Rutherford's experiments, most of the electrons went right through their targets without interacting. A few, however, bounced back at sharp angles. An analysis of the scattering pattern of the electrons indicated that there were three hard lumps inside the proton. Experiments repeated at CERN gave about the same results. While some physicists do not consider this a clear demonstration of the existence of quarks, it certainly is strong evidence in favor of the quark model. Jerome L. Friedman (1930–), Henry W. Kendall (1926–), and Richard E. Taylor (1929–), the leaders of the team working at Stanford, shared the 1990 Nobel Prize in physics for this discovery.

QUARK COLOR

There was one final objection to the quark model. Quarks are spin-$\tfrac{1}{2}$ particles, and are therefore fermions. But fermions obey the Pauli exclusion principle, which says that no two fermions, such as electrons, can occupy the same quantum state. The omega minus particle, though, is composed of three strange quarks, which are fermions, each with identical spin (a quantum state) of $\tfrac{1}{2}$. This is certainly a violation of the Pauli principle.

A *diagram of the structure of an atom. An atom consists of one or more electrons that orbit around a tiny, central nucleus. The nucleus is made of protons (red) and neutrons (blue). Each proton and neutron consists of three quarks.*

In 1964 the American physicist Oscar Greenberg (1932–) suggested that quarks must carry yet another quantum number that is different for the three strange quarks. He said that quarks come in three different "colors": "red," "green," and "blue." The colors, of course, are not real, but they do express some new quantum property of quarks. To make an omega minus particle, then, we take one strange quark of each color and, presto, they are no longer identical. The idea of quark color has been tremendously fruitful.

GLUONS   The force carrier between quarks is the gluon. It is a zero-mass particle with no electric charge, similar to the photon, the carrier of the electric force. And just as protons and electrons have an electric charge, quarks are said to have a color charge. To emphasize the importance of color in the interaction of quarks, the strong force is sometimes called the color force. Unlike photons, however, which do not have any electric charge, and neither attract nor repel each other, gluons themselves are also colored, and interact with each other.

The theory of how quarks interact is called quantum chromodynamics, or QCD. The name is derived from the Greek word *chroma*, meaning "color." According to this theory, the strong force is transmitted by eight different varieties of gluons. Some gluons can change the color of the quark they interact with. A blue quark, for example, can absorb a gluon and become a green quark. In spite of the obvious complexity of gluon interactions, QCD does provide a good description of how the strong force affects quarks.

Although gluons, like quarks, have never been directly observed, there is a great deal of indirect experimental evidence for their existence.

THE NOVEMBER REVOLUTION   In spite of the many successes of the quark model, the inability to find a free quark continued to disturb many physicists. Strangely enough, what provided more evidence for the quark model was the discovery, in 1974, of a new meson, the psi meson.

It was found simultaneously by two different groups, one led by Samuel Chao Ching Ting (1936–) at Brookhaven National Laboratory and the other led by Burton Richter (1931–) at the Stanford Linear Accelerator. Ting and Richter shared the Nobel Prize in physics in 1976 for their discovery.

The date of the discovery was November 11, 1974, and the events that followed were so dramatic that it has often been called the November

Leon Lederman, director of the Fermilab, helped to discover the fifth quark flavor.

Revolution. In the attempts to explain some of the unusual properties of this new particle, such as its extremely long lifetime, the quark model won the day. Part of the revolution was that a new quark flavor, called charm, was required to explain the properties of the psi meson.

Soon other experiments turned up new hadrons that were shown to contain the charmed quark, and the theory of quarks was finally universally accepted by scientists.

In 1977 a team led by Leon Lederman, director of the Fermilab in Chicago, discovered a fifth quark flavor, the "b" quark, named either *beauty* or *bottom*. There is strong theoretical and experimental evidence for yet another quark flavor, the "t" quark, for either *top* or *truth*. In April 1994, an international team of more than 400 scientists working at the Fermilab announced that they had found the elusive quark. The top quark is very heavy, almost as heavy as an atom of platinum. This means that enormous amounts of energy are required to create it in the laboratory, and is one of the reasons it has proven so hard to find.

THE STANDARD MODEL   After 2,000 years of searching for the ultimate, indivisible constituents of matter, scientists have now arrived at the view that all matter is made up of three kinds of elementary particles: leptons, quarks, and force carriers. This is called the Standard Model.

The particles that make up this fundamental scheme of nature are sum-

PARTICLE TREE

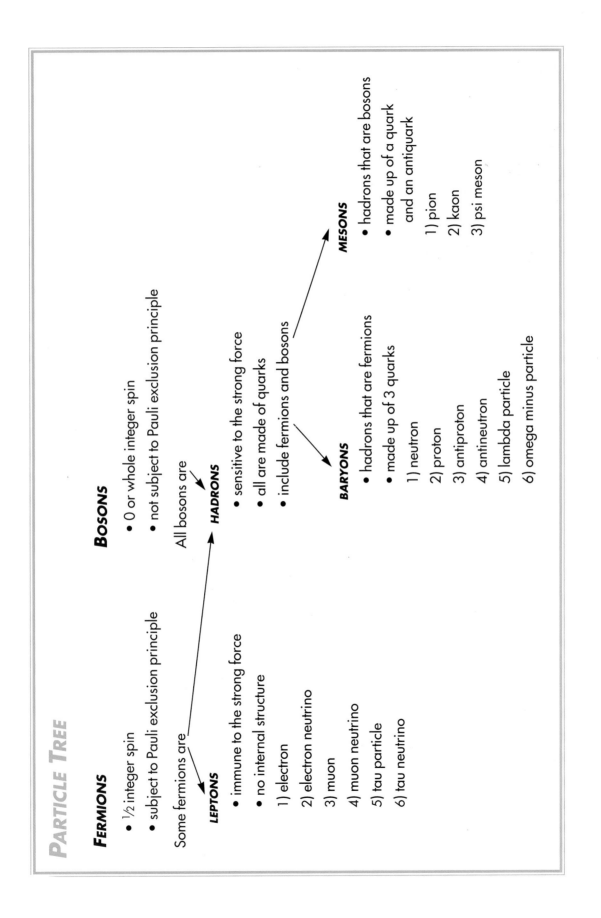

FERMIONS
- ½ integer spin
- subject to Pauli exclusion principle

Some fermions are

LEPTONS
- immune to the strong force
- no internal structure

1) electron
2) electron neutrino
3) muon
4) muon neutrino
5) tau particle
6) tau neutrino

BOSONS
- 0 or whole integer spin
- not subject to Pauli exclusion principle

All bosons are

HADRONS
- sensitive to the strong force
- all are made of quarks
- include fermions and bosons

BARYONS
- hadrons that are fermions
- made up of 3 quarks

1) neutron
2) proton
3) antiproton
4) antineutron
5) lambda particle
6) omega minus particle

MESONS
- hadrons that are bosons
- made up of a quark and an antiquark

1) pion
2) kaon
3) psi meson

marized below. For simplicity, the antiparticle of each of the particles shown in the table is omitted. The names of the antiparticles are simply constructed by placing the prefix *anti* in front of the name of the particle. The antiparticle of the muon, for example, is the antimuon. The only antiparticle that has an individual name is the positron, the antiparticle of the electron.

LEPTONS	QUARKS		FORCE	FORCE CARRIER (exchange particle)
electron	up		gravity	graviton
electron neutrino	down		electric	photon
muon	charm		weak	intermediate vector bosons (3 kinds)
muon neutrino	strange		strong	
tau particle	top/truth			gluons (8 varieties)
tau neutrino	bottom/beauty			

The goal of finally arriving at relatively "few" building blocks of matter seems somewhat elusive. If we add up all these elementary particles, remembering that every lepton and quark listed above has an antiparticle and that each of the quarks come in three different colors, we arrive at 12 leptons, 36 quarks, and 13 force carriers. A total of 61 particles!

There is yet another fundamental particle, called the Higgs boson. This particle is named after Peter Higgs (1929–) of the University of Edinburgh, Scotland. The particle has never been seen, but is one of the major trophies sought by many teams of particle hunters all over the world. The search for the Higgs boson was to have been one of the central tasks of the recently aborted Superconducting Super Collider (SSC) that was to have been built in Texas.

The importance of the Higgs boson is that it explains the long-standing riddle of why the carriers of the weak force, the W and Z particles, are so massive, while the carriers of the other forces have no mass. According to one of the most successful of modern theories, called the electroweak theory, the Higgs particle "creates" mass by the way it couples to the weak exchange particles.

QUARK GENERATIONS   In spite of the large number of fundamental particles, many physicists are heartened by the thought that many of the

*P*eter Higgs predicted the existence
of another fundamental particle,
the Higgs boson.

*C*onstruction has been halted
at the gigantic uperconducting
Super Collider in Texas.
Particle hunters will need to
use other particle accelerators
in their search for the Higgs
boson.

particles are related to one another in some way. They even speak of families
or generations of quarks and leptons.

If we focus on the particles that make up ordinary atoms and matter in
the world around us, only two quarks and one lepton are required. The up
and down quarks are sufficient to make neutrons and protons, and if we add
the electron (a lepton), we have the parts of the atom. We still require gluons
to bind the quarks together and photons to transmit the electric force that
holds electrons near the nucleus of an atom, but this is still a manageable
number. This is often called the first generation of quarks and leptons.

The second generation includes the strange and charmed quarks, and
deals with matter seen only in accelerators or cosmic rays. The third genera-

tion adds the top and bottom quarks, and here again explains exotic particles found only at high energies.

THE FUTURE   What comes next? The search for the fundamental building blocks of matter has been somewhat like peeling an onion. Scientific investigation has changed the focus from continuous matter, to atoms, to the nucleus, to protons and neutrons, and finally to quarks. Some physicists wonder if there isn't still another, deeper layer to be exposed. The sixty-odd particles that make up the Standard Model seem too numerous to be truly "fundamental."

The search for simplicity continues, and there are theories being discussed that suggest that quarks and leptons, too, might have some internal composition. The hope is always to build a complex world out of just a few simple parts.

It may take years before the next layer of matter, if it exists, comes into view. Or perhaps some new idea or theory, such as the grand unification theory, trying to show that the four forces really stem from a single force, might simplify our understanding of matter with a brilliant new insight. Only time will tell.

FOR FURTHER READING

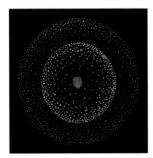

Apfel, Necia. *It's All Relative*. New York: Lothrop, 1981.

Asimov, Isaac. *How Did We Find Out About Atoms*. New York: Walker and Co., 1976.

Averous, Pierre. *The Atom*. New York: Barron, 1988.

Biel, Timothy Levi. *Atoms: Building Blocks of Matter*. San Diego: Greenhaven, 1990.

Goldenstern, Joyce. *Albert Einstein: Physicist and Genius*. Hillside, N.J.: Enslow Pubs., 1994.

Hammontree, Marie. *Albert Einstein: Young Thinker*. New York: Aladdin, 1986.

Ireland, Karin. *Albert Einstein*. Morristown, N.J.: Silver Burdett, 1989.

Lafferty, Peter. *Albert Einstein*. New York: Franklin Watts, 1992.

McGowen, Tom. *Radioactivity: From the Curies to the Atomic Age*. New York: Franklin Watts, 1988.

Milne, Lorus J., and Margery Milne. *Understanding Radioactivity*. New York: Atheneum, 1989.

Quigg, Chris. "Elementary Particles and Forces," *Scientific American*, April 1985, 84–95.

Swisher, Clarice. *Relativity: Opposing Viewpoints*. San Diego: Greenhaven, 1990.

Tauber, Gerald E. *Relativity: From Einstein to Black Holes*. New York: Franklin Watts, 1988.

THE PERIODIC TABLE OF ELEMENTS

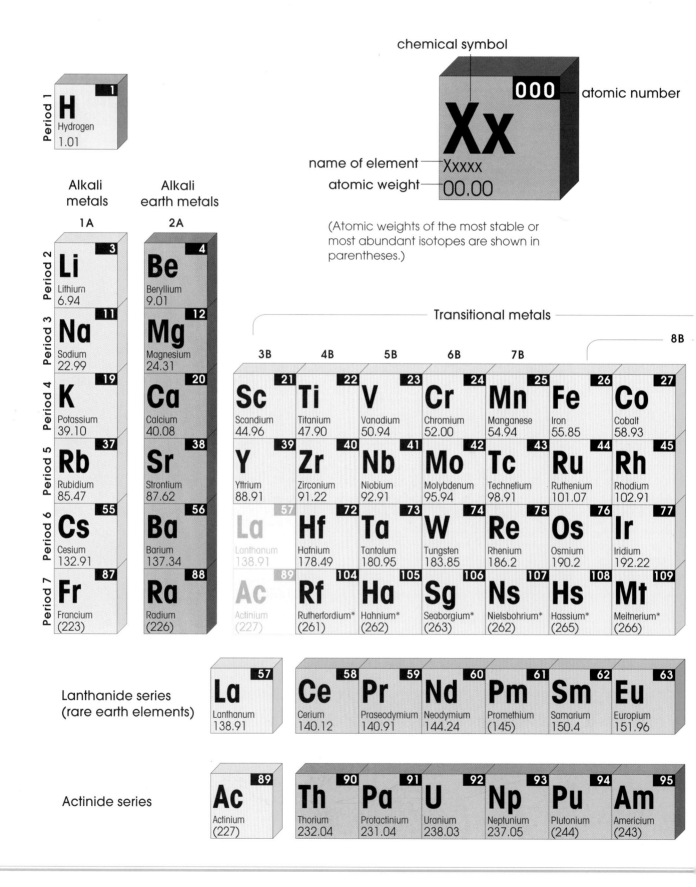

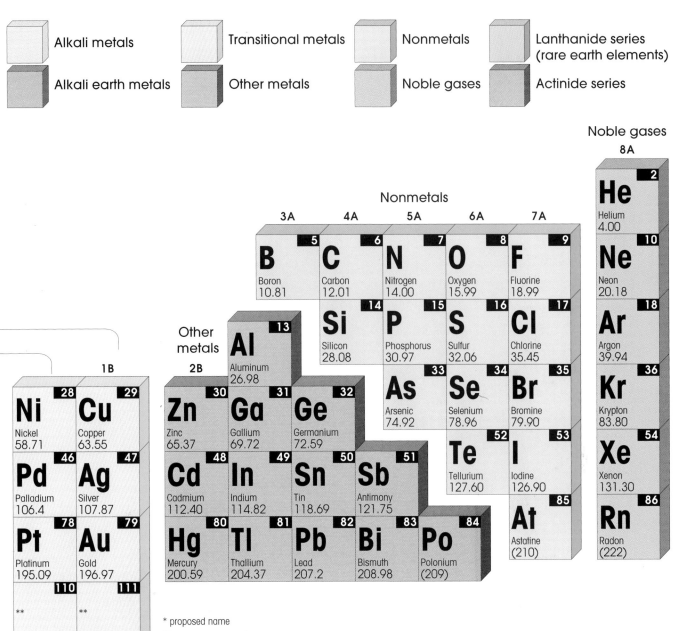

Alkali metals

Alkali earth metals

Transitional metals

Other metals

Nonmetals

Noble gases

Lanthanide series (rare earth elements)

Actinide series

Noble gases
8A

Nonmetals

| 3A | 4A | 5A | 6A | 7A |

He 2 — Helium 4.00

B 5 — Boron 10.81
C 6 — Carbon 12.01
N 7 — Nitrogen 14.00
O 8 — Oxygen 15.99
F 9 — Fluorine 18.99
Ne 10 — Neon 20.18

Si 14 — Silicon 28.08
P 15 — Phosphorus 30.97
S 16 — Sulfur 32.06
Cl 17 — Chlorine 35.45
Ar 18 — Argon 39.94

As 33 — Arsenic 74.92
Se 34 — Selenium 78.96
Br 35 — Bromine 79.90
Kr 36 — Krypton 83.80

Te 52 — Tellurium 127.60
I 53 — Iodine 126.90
Xe 54 — Xenon 131.30

At 85 — Astatine (210)
Rn 86 — Radon (222)

Other metals

Al 13 — Aluminum 26.98

1B

Ni 28 — Nickel 58.71
Cu 29 — Copper 63.55

2B

Zn 30 — Zinc 65.37
Ga 31 — Gallium 69.72
Ge 32 — Germanium 72.59

Pd 46 — Palladium 106.4
Ag 47 — Silver 107.87

Cd 48 — Cadmium 112.40
In 49 — Indium 114.82
Sn 50 — Tin 118.69
Sb 51 — Antimony 121.75

Pt 78 — Platinum 195.09
Au 79 — Gold 196.97

Hg 80 — Mercury 200.59
Tl 81 — Thallium 204.37
Pb 82 — Lead 207.2
Bi 83 — Bismuth 208.98
Po 84 — Polonium (209)

110 **
111 **

* proposed name
** no name proposed

Gd 64 — Gadolinium 157.25
Tb 65 — Terbium 158.93
Dy 66 — Dysprosium 162.50
Ho 67 — Holmium 164.93
Er 68 — Erbium 167.26
Tm 69 — Thulium 168.93
Yb 70 — Ytterbium 173.04
Lu 71 — Lutetium 174.97

Cm 96 — Curium (247)
Bk 97 — Berkelium (247)
Cf 98 — Californium (251)
Es 99 — Einsteinium (254)
Fm 100 — Fermium (257)
Md 101 — Mendelevium (258)
No 102 — Nobelium (255)
Lr 103 — Lawrencium (256)

PARTICLE GUIDE

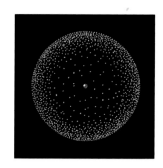

alpha particle—A helium nucleus, consisting of two protons and two neutrons, that is emitted by certain radioactive atoms undergoing a process known as alpha decay.

antiparticle—Every particle in nature has a corresponding antiparticle, which has the same mass as the particle but an opposite electric charge. When a particle and its corresponding antiparticle come in contact, they "annihilate" each other and produce energy.

baryon—A member of the family of hadrons that is also a fermion. All the baryons are made up of three quarks.

beta particles—An early name for electrons.

bosons—The family of particles that have a spin that is either 0 or a whole number, e.g., 1, 2, 3. A photon with a spin of 0 and a $W+$ or $W-$ particle with a spin of 1 are examples of bosons.

cosmic ray particles—High-energy particles originating in outer space that are constantly bombarding Earth. They consist mainly of protons.

electron—A negatively charged particle that is one of the subatomic particles that make up an atom. Electrons are one of the six particles known as leptons.

exchange particle—A particle that acts as a messenger to transmit a force. The exchange particle that transmits the electric force, for example, is the photon, while the exchange particle that transmits the strong force is the gluon.

fermions—The family of particles with a half-integer spin, e.g., $\frac{1}{2}$, $\frac{3}{2}$, $\frac{5}{2}$. Electrons, protons, and neutrons are examples of fermions. Fermions are subject to the Pauli exclusion principle.

gluon—The particle that is exchanged between quarks to transmit the strong nuclear force.

graviton—The exchange particle that transmits the force of gravity between two objects. It has never been directly observed.

hadrons—Particles that are sensitive to the strong force. All hadrons are made up of quarks. Three quarks, two "up" and one "down," for example, form a hadron known as the proton.

Higgs boson—A particle whose existence is theoretically predicted. It has never been observed, but particle hunters around the world are making an enormous effort to identify it. The existence of the Higgs boson would explain why the carriers of the weak force are so massive, while the carriers of the other forces have no mass.

intermediate vector bosons—A name given to the carriers of the weak force, the $W+$, $W-$, and $Z°$ particles.

kaon—A meson that was the first of a number of particles called strange particles found in cosmic rays. They were called strange because the particles all lived for a relatively long time before decaying into other particles.

lambda particle—A "strange" baryon, strange because it has an unusually long lifetime. It behaves in many ways like a heavy neutron.

leptons—Elementary particles that are not sensitive to the strong force. They appear to have no structure, and so are thought of as being truly fundamental. They all have a spin of $\frac{1}{2}$, and so are fermions. An electron is an important example of a lepton.

mesons—Any hadron that is a boson. An example is the pion. Mesons are made up of a quark and an antiquark.

muons—A charged lepton with a mass approximately 200 times that of an electron. It is unstable, and the negatively charged muon, for example, quickly decays into an electron neutrino and a muon neutrino.

neutrino—A particle thought to be massless, emitted in certain kinds of radioactive decay. It is electrically neutral and a lepton. There are three different kinds of neutrinos: the electron neutrino, the muon neutrino, and the tau neutrino. Each of these neutrinos also has its antiparticle.

neutron—One of the particles that exist in the nuclei of atoms. It is electrically neutral and made up of three quarks.

omega minus particle—A heavy baryon whose discovery confirmed the Eightfold Way.

photon—A particle of light energy. It is also the carrier of the electric force.

pion—A particle that is the lightest meson. It was first predicted theoretically by the Japanese physicist Hideki Yukawa, who thought of it as the carrier of the strong force.

positron—The antiparticle of the electron. It has the same mass as the electron, but has a positive charge.

proton—A positively charged particle in the nucleus of all atoms. It is made up of three quarks.

psi meson—A heavy meson whose discovery in November 1974 stunned the world of physics. It led to the discovery of a fourth quark flavor, called charm.

quarks—The most basic building blocks of all matter. There are six types of quarks.

strange particle—A particle containing a strange quark.

tau particle—An extremely massive lepton with a mass nearly double that of a proton. It is unstable, carries an electric charge, and is associated with its own neutrino, the tau neutrino.

valence electrons—The outermost electrons of an atom. These electrons often determine the chemical behavior of the element.

GLOSSARY

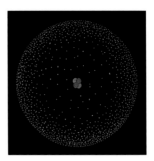

angular momentum—A measure of how difficult it is to stop a rotating or spinning object.

antimatter—Matter that is composed of antiparticles.

atom—The basic unit of an element that retains its identity during chemical reactions.

atomic mass unit (amu)—A unit of mass that is exactly equal to one-twelfth the mass of carbon 12, one of the isotopes of carbon.

atomic number—The number of protons in the nucleus of an atom. It determines the charge on the nucleus.

atomic theory—The branch of science dealing with the basic structure of atoms. Its final goal is to explain the structure of all matter.

atomic weight—The average mass of the atoms in a naturally occurring element expressed in atomic mass units.

beta decay—A form of radioactivity in which a neutron is transformed into a proton. At the same time, an energetic electron, or beta particle, is emitted along with an antineutrino.

Brownian motion—The irregular motion of microscopically small particles suspended in a liquid. The motion is caused by the random collisions of the atoms or molecules of the liquid with the particles.

cathode rays—The stream of electrons emitted by the negative electrode (cathode) in a gaseous discharge tube.

charm—One of the characteristics of quarks.

chemistry—The science that studies the properties of substances and how they react with one another.

color—The name given to one of the quantum numbers assigned to quarks. Quarks come in three colors.

compound—A substance composed of two or more elements that are combined by chemical bonds.

conservation of energy—One of the fundamental principles of nature, which states that the sum total of energy in any closed system always remains constant.

Eightfold Way—A method of classifying particles that was introduced by Nobel Prize-winning physicist Murray Gell-Mann in 1961. The name is taken from Buddhist scripture.

Einstein's theory of relativity—Usually refers to the special theory of relativity published by Albert Einstein in 1905. It roughly states that all the laws of physics are the same in equivalent frames of reference. One of the consequences of this is the equivalence of mass and energy, expressed in the equation $E = mc^2$.

electroweak theory—A successful scientific theory that describes how the electric force and the weak force behave. It is of fundamental importance in the description of subatomic particles.

element—A substance that cannot be decomposed into simpler substances by chemical or physical means.

flavor—A word used to define the various kinds of quarks. It was first used by Murray Gell-Mann when he suggested that there were several types of quarks. His way of stating this was to say that quarks come in several flavors.

frequency—The number of waves that pass a certain point every second.

gamma rays—High-energy photons emitted by the nucleus of an atom. They resemble X rays.

grand unification theory—An ambitious theory put forward by some physicists that attempts to unify all the forces. It attempts to demonstrate that the four known forces all stem from a single force.

Heisenberg uncertainty principle—A fundamental principle first put forward by Werner Heisenberg in 1927. It states that it is impossible to simultaneously measure both the energy and time of a system with absolute precision. This also implies that the greater the mass of an exchange particle, the shorter its range. There are other sets of variables, such as position and momentum, for which this is also true. The uncertainty follows from the fact that matter has a wave character.

ion—An atom that has an electric charge. An ion is usually made by removing electrons from or adding electrons to an atom.

isotopes—Atoms of the same element that have different numbers of neutrons and therefore have different weights.

magnetic field—A region of space where a moving electric charge will experience a force. Magnetic fields can be created by permanent magnets or by electric current.

mass—The quantity of matter in an object.

meteorology—A branch of science that studies the atmosphere and the various factors that affect weather.

molecule—A group of two or more atoms that are bonded together. The atoms that make up the molecule can be of the same or different elements. A molecule is the smallest unit of any compound.

Moseley's law—A law that relates the wavelength of the X rays emitted by an element in an X-ray tube and its atomic number.

nuclear accelerator—A machine designed to accelerate particles such as electrons and protons to high speeds and energies. These speeding particles are then smashed into one another or into some barrier to probe the structure of other particles.

nuclear atom—The model of the atom in which all the atom's positive charge is localized in a small, dense nucleus at the center of the atom.

nuclear reactor—A device used to extract and utilize the energy given off by the fissioning of uranium isotopes.

orbit—The path taken by a particle such as an electron as it circles about the nucleus of an atom.

particle hunters—Scientists engaged in research whose goal is to discover and identify new subatomic particles.

Pauli exclusion principle—The principle that states that no more than one fermion, such as an electron, can occupy the same quantum state at the same time.

periodic table of the elements—A chart showing all the elements arranged in such a way that elements in the same column have similar chemical properties.

photoelectric effect—The emission of electrons from a metal when the metal is illuminated with light whose photons have sufficient energy to eject electrons.

physics—The science that describes the principles that govern the observed phenomena in the physical universe.

Planck's constant—A physical constant relating the energy of a photon to its frequency.

planetary model—A model of the atom that assumes the electrons orbit about the nucleus in a fashion similar to the way planets orbit the Sun.

quanta—The plural of *quantum*. It refers to the fact that light energy comes in small "packages," called quanta.

quantum chromodynamics—A theory that describes the behavior and characteristics of the strong force.

quantum numbers—Numbers generated in the solution of the Schrödinger equation that define the shape and size of the electron "clouds" surrounding the nucleus of an atom.

quantum theory—The modern theory of the atom, based on the wave behavior of matter.

radioactivity—The spontaneous disintegration or decay of the nucleus of an atom to form a different nucleus. Particles and energy are usually emitted as a result of the process.

Schrödinger equation—The fundamental equation at the heart of quantum mechanics. Its solution supplies information about atomic and nuclear systems.

shell—The family of electrons orbiting the nucleus of an atom that all have the same principal quantum number.

spectral lines—The colors given off by an element when it is heated. Each element emits a different set of colors, which then can be used to identify the element.

spin—A term used to indicate that such particles as electrons, neutrons, and protons all behave as if they were spinning balls of charge. Spin indicates that the particle has angular momentum.

Standard Model—A theory that states that all the particles observed in the universe can be constructed from only six leptons and six quarks. It also states that there are four basic forces, all transmitted between objects by exchange particles.

strong force—The force holding the nucleus of an atom together. It is transmitted by the exchange of gluons between quarks.

suspension—The dispersion of microscopic particles throughout a liquid.

transmutation of the elements—Refers to the fact that radioactivity is accompanied by one element changing or "transmuting" into another element.

wave theory of light—A theory that states that light is transmitted through space in the form of a wave.

weak force—The force responsible for radioactivity. It has three exchange particles, $W+$, $W-$, and $Z°$.

PHOTO NOTE

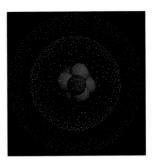

The chapter opening pages and certain backmatter pages are decorated with uncaptioned photographs. Here's a key describing those pictures:

False-color bubble chamber and cloud chamber photographs:

page 5: A cosmic ray muon (green) knocks out an atomic electron (red).

page 9: A single electron forms a spiral track in a magnetic field.

page 15: The symmetrical production of matter and antimatter.

page 23: The production and decay of a lambda particle.

page 35: A cosmic ray sulfur nucleus (red) collides with a nucleus in a photographic emulsion.

page 43: A positron (red) knocks out an atomic electron (green). Although they do interact, the positron and electron do not come close enough to annihilate each other.

page 49: A proton (red) scatters other protons (also red). The blue particle tracks are not involved.

page 55: The difference between the tracks of a proton (red) and an alpha particle (yellow).

page 69: The annihilation of matter and antimatter: an antiproton (pale blue) meets a proton.

Computer-generated graphics:

page 83: Hydrogen. A proton (red) is surrounded by an electron cloud.

page 86: Helium. The nucleus (2 protons, 2 neutrons) is surrounded by its electron cloud.

page 89: Beryllium. The nucleus (4 protons, 5 neutrons) is surrounded by two electron shells.

page 93: Beryllium. The nucleus and two electron orbitals are shown.

page 94: Lithium. The nucleus is shown in red. The yellow cloud represents the first electron orital, with the second orbital cloud colored blue.

INDEX

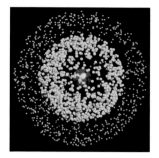

alpha particles, 20, 21, 22, 23, 24, 28, 29
angular momentum, 39, 40, 41, 46, 47, 51, 57
antineutron, 62, 79
antiparticles, 61, 62, 63, 64, 80
antiproton, 62, 70, 79
antiquarks, 73, 74, 79
atomic bombs, 55
atomic mass units (amu), 27, 28, 31
atomic number, 25, 27, 28, 29, 30, 31, 53, 57
atomic theory, 49, 61
atoms, 5, 6–9, 10, *10*, 31, *76*, 81. *See also* electrons; neutrons; protons.
  behavior of, 11
  and Bohr theory, 49
  defining, 25
  model of, 32, 43
  modern picture of, 29
  neutrality of, 26
  nuclear, 24, 28
  nucleus of, 30, 56
  properties of, 33, 55
  radioactive, 22, 23
  splitting, 8, 15, 17
  structure of, 13
  unstable, 21

baryons, 70, 71, 72, 74
Becquerel, Antoine-Henri, 19, 20

beta decay, 56, 57, 58
beta particles, 20, 21, 32, 57
Bohr, Niels, 39, *40*, 41, 43, 45, 49
bosons, 69, 70, 79
Brookhaven National Laboratory, 65, *66*, 71, 72, 77
Brownian motion, 9, 10
Brown, Robert, 9

Cavendish Laboratory, 15, 20, 29
Chamberlain, Owen, 62, *63*
cosmic rays, 61, 64, 65, 66, 81
Curie, Irène, 29, *30*
Curie, Marie, 19, 20, *20*, 29
Curie, Pierre, 20, *20*, 29

Dalton, John, 6, *7*, 8
de Broglie, Louis, 45, *46*, 49

Eightfold Way, 71, 72
Einstein, Albert, 9, 10, 36, *37*, 37, 39, 44, 45, 52, 55, 61, 62
electric charges, 15, 46, 77
electric force, 58, 59, 60, 77, 80
electricity, 16, 17, 56
electrodes, 15, 16, 18
electron clouds, 50
electrons, 13, 15, 16, 17, 19, 24, *25*, 43, 44, 45, 46, 50, *50*
  and atoms, 32, 33, 39, 49, 52, 53, 55, 60, 70

and beta decay, 58
and elements, 27, 29, 31
emitting, 21, 37, 38
and energy, 64
and leptons, 81
and muons, 65, 69
and neutrinos, 66
and photons, 62
and radioactivity, 57
and spin, 47, 58
and subatomic particles, 30
electroweak theory, 80
Ernst, Max Karl, 36
exchange particles, 60, 61, 64, 80
exclusion principle, 52, 53, 69, 75,
    79

Fermi, Enrico, 58, *59*, 59, 69
Fermilab, *78*, 78
fermions, 69, 70, 75, 79
fission, 58
force carriers, 78, 80

gamma rays, 20, 21
Geiger counter, 23
Gell-Mann, Murray, 71, *72*, 72, 73
gluons, 60, 65, 77, 80, 81
grand unification theory, 82
graviton, 60, 80
gravity, 56, 59, 60, 80

hadrons, 70, 71, 72, 73, 74, 75, 79
Heisenberg uncertainty principle, 64
Heisenberg, Werner Karl, 64
Higgs boson, 80
Higgs, Peter, 80, *81*

intermediate vector bosons, 61, 80

Joliot-Curie, Frédéric, 29, *30*

kaon, 66, 79

lambda particle, 66, 67, 79
Lederman, Leon M., 65, *78*, 78
leptons, 70, 71, 78, 79, 80, 81, 82

Mendeleév, Dimitri Ivanovitch, 11, 12, 72
mesons, 70, 71, 72, 74, 77
Moseley, Henry Gwyn-Jeffreys, 25, 26,
    26, 27
muons, 65, 69, 70, 79, 80

neutrinos, 58, 59, 63, 65, 70, 79, 80
neutrons, 29, 45, *76*, 82
    and antiparticles, 63
    and atoms, 55
    and beta decay, 58
    and elements, 31
    and nuclear reactions, 59
    and quarks, 75, 81
    and spin, 47, 57, 69
    and strong force, 56, 70
    and subatomic particles, 20
November Revolution, 77, 78
nuclear atom, 24, 28, 32, 75
nuclear power, 8, 61
nucleus, *25*, *31*, *50*, *76*, 82
    atoms, 24, 26, 32, 43, 56, 69
    and angular momentum, 41
    and beta decay, 58
    and elements, 25, 28, 29, 31, 53
    and electrons, 39, 45, 49, 51, 52, 57
    and gluons, 60

omega minus particle, 72, 75, 77, 79

Pauli, Wolfgang, 52, *52*, 53, 58, 65, 69,
    75, 79
periodic table, 11, 12, 17, 26, 27, 29,
    32, 52, 53, 69, 72

photoelectric effect, 37
photons, 36, 38, 39, 43, 44, 45, 47, 60,
    62, 63, 64, 69, 77, 80
pions, 64, 65, 66, 69, 70, 79
Planck, Ludwig, 36, *37*
Planck's constant, 36, 38, 39, 40, 46
positron, 61, *62*, 62, 63, 64, 80
Powell, Cecil Frank, 64, 65, 66
protons, 28, 29, 45, 74, *74*, 82
    and atoms, 32, 55, 60
    and elements, 31
    and neutrinos, 66
    nuclear, 39
    and nucleus, 56
    and quarks, 75, 81
    and radioactivity, 56–57
    and spin, 58, 69, 70
    and subatomic particles, 30
    and weak force, 61
psi meson, 77, 78, 79

quantum chromodynamics (QCD), 77
quantum energy, 36,
quantum mechanics, 33, 61, 64
quantum numbers, 50, 51, 52, 53, 77
quantum theory, 39, 46, 49, 60
quark flavors, 73, 78
quarks, 56, 60, 67, 70, 73, 81, 82
    model of, 74, *74*
    and neutrons and protons, 75
    strange, 73, 75, 77, 81

radioactive elements, 11, 19, 20, 22, 23,
    27, 28
radioactivity, 19–23, 28–29. *See also*
    beta decay.

Röntgen, Wilhelm Conrad, 18, *18*
Rutherford, Ernest, 20, 21, *21*, 22, 23,
    24, 28, 75

Schrödinger, Erwin, 49, 50, *51*, 61
spectral lines, 43, 44, 47
spin, 46, 47, 50, 51, 53, 57, 58, 69, 70,
    71, 75, 79
Standard Model, 78, 82
strange particles, 67
strong force, 56, 58, 59, 60, 64, 65, 70,
    77, 79, 80
subatomic particles, 30, 49, 55, 66
Superconducting Super Collider, *81*

tau particle, 70, 79, 80
theory of relativity, 33, 52, 55, 61
Thomson, Sir Joseph John, 13, 15, *16*,
    16, 17, 27
transmutation, 22

valence electrons, 53

W particles, 61, 80
wavelengths, 25, 41, 43
waves, 35, 36, 39, 45, 46, 49, 51, 52, 53
weak force, 58, 59, 60, 61, 80

X rays, 18, *19*, 21, 25, 38, 45
X-ray tube, 25

Yukawa, Hideki, 64, 65

Z° particles, *60*, 61, 80